Life in Eternity

Life in Eternity

Robin Oake

Life in Eternity - a memoir

Published by The Conrad Press Ltd. in the United Kingdom 2023

Tel: +44(0)1227 472 874

www.theconradpress.com

info@theconradpress.com

ISBN 978-1-915494-85-6

Typesetting and Cover Design by: Charlotte Mouncey, www.bookstyle.co.uk

The Conrad Press logo was designed by Maria Priestley.

Printed and bound in Great Britain by Clays Ltd, Elcograf S.p.A.

This book is dedicated to the memory of DC
Stephen Robin Oake QGM (21st April 1962 - 14th January
2003), killed as a detective with the Greater Manchester
Police while on duty in an anti-terrorist operation.

His Christian life called him to serve.

Contents

A biographical note about the author

Robin Oake joined the Metropolitan Police at the age of nineteen. Following a three-month training period he was posted as a constable to St John's Wood, north-west London. After three years he was invited to serve at New Scotland Yard and during this time married Chris, a nurse at St Thomas's Hospital – they had three lovely children – Stephen, Judith and Sue - and following that, having passed the Sergeant's examination, served in London's West End including Soho.

Next he became a Firearms Officer. He was promoted to Station Sergeant and was an Instructor at the Training School. He was selected to be an Inspector and on a course at Bramshill College, passed and awarded a scholarship to University College, London where he read law. After gaining his degree, he was awarded it by Her Majesty the Queen Mother who simply said, 'Now back to the real work, Mr Oake!'

As an Inspector he was in 'A' Division, the centre of the Metropolitan Police with Buckingham Palace, the Houses of Parliament, and other well-known situations especially as the Division was targeted with bombs! Promoted to Chief Inspector in Brixton Division, a diverse and very busy district but after two years was invited to join the staff at Bramshill Police College in Hampshire principally studying counter terrorism.

After two very busy years at Bramshill, Robin was invited to serve in Greater Manchester in the rank of Superintendent and that included two years in Moss Side before the next promotion to Chief Superintendent following a Senior Command Course and time in Miami, USA and after a further two years in Manchester he was appointed Assistant Chief Constable. An invitation came from the Isle of Man to come for interview from which he was appointed Chief Constable to a Force which needed much updating. After thirteen years he retired and, returning to England, he worked in London as a senior officer in the Order of St John before retirement.

His son, Steve, a detective by now, was unfortunately killed while on duty during a terrorist incident. Robin Oake's Christian faith was well known in the Forces where he served and in which he also conducted a steady stream of speaking engagements. There is a Wikipedia page devoted to the late Steve Oake which makes his great bravery and courageous sacrifice extremely clear. https://en.wikipedia.org/wiki/Murder_of_Stephen_Oake

Robin Oake says: I would add here that the news of Steve's death came from Greater Manchester Police – by telephone – and I was alone at home in the Isle of Man. Chris, my wife, was in Altrincham looking after grandchildren while Sue was in hospital and I had to tell Chris before she saw it on TV. I had always said to colleagues, 'never give bad news by telephone – you never know what the reaction would be.' I then heard that the Press had chartered a flight to the Isle of Man so I set up a press conference in our newest Police Station at Port Erin. There were more than fifty reporters in attendance who, I felt, were very understanding and non-confrontational. Then one respected reporter stood and asked (I am sure with no malice at all), 'Mr Oake, what do you think of the man who killed your son?' Wow! Quite a question. I thought for a moment and silently prayed for wisdom. Then, looking him in the eye, I simply said, 'I don't know the man but I forgive him and pray that God will forgive him.' Boy, did that cause a loud stir, shouts and reporters all wanting something further from me. Tactfully, I tried to calm the conference by saying, 'There will be a full enquiry into the incident and, no doubt, Court proceedings. Meanwhile, my concern is for Lesley, Steve's lovely wife, his three children; for Steve's two sisters and, above all, my wife.' The Press made a lot of my remark and I had some helpful comments from my senior colleagues in other Forces but especially from Sir James Anderton, Chief Constable of Greater Manchester, a lovely Christian man.

Other books published by the author:

With God on the Streets (Authentic Media)

Father, Forgive (Authentic Media)

The Power of Powerlessness (10 Publishing)

NOTE: This book is for everyone, and especially for Christians (and people who aren't) – and especially Christians in the ministry – both for our own walk and for our willingness and ability to witness about our faith and tell others about the reasons we have for our faith.

Preface

What you are about to read comes with a serious 'health' warning!

We live in days where political correctness rules the day and night and to accost someone – especially if you don't know them – and begin to tell them about Jesus and their need of a Saviour is just not on – generally speaking. Sadly, but it is true, there's an assumption by some ministers and others in leadership that everyone who attends church services is a Christian, a believer in the Bible and living an upright life.

Very sadly, because of that, there is limited power in the local church and a host of people heading in the wrong direction – probably very nice and upright people – and therefore not willing to display a full Christian commitment. Because of that, not living for and speaking out for the Saviour, thousands – including many sports e.g. soccer, rugby, cricket, tennis tournaments and so on – watch the matches but are spectators as opposed to players. Sadly, I guess a huge number of people attend their local church, cathedral, mission hall etc. but have not made a whole-hearted commitment to the Lord Jesus and while they enjoy the friendship of others who attend the church, a fully committed life following conversion may not have ever occurred to them as necessary! Please, this is an observation because I know many, many folk who are active church attenders and members whose Christian lives are a real joy to know – and powerfully effective!

I am not being timid by being critical– just tactfully careful. In the dream which is outlined in the first chapter, there were no such barriers or warnings. All I had in my disturbed sleep were the shouts and sense of being accosted so that I couldn't move because of a dense crowed condemning me, shouting angrily, 'You didn't tell me'. The dream was absolutely right in one sense for there are probably hundreds of people to whom I could and should have spoken about the Lord Jesus but for some reason I never did.

I guess that in years gone by, when we were known as a Christian country, our laws, in the main, aligned with Christian principles. Obviously one should never - at least, one hopes - have been crude in public places such as Hyde Park Speakers Corner as some speakers are or, as was once quite common, on street corners in towns but a direct challenge to non church-goers or unbelievers was not condemned though, albeit, mostly ignored.

But things have changed and in our multi-faith country and where Christianity is not adopted by the majority and where it is easy to seem rude or judgmental by proclaiming the Christian message - care, quite rightly, has to be taken. Modern society now has a different perspective on life, on privacy, or on multi-cultural differences - all of which affect the way we live and, in the context of this, how we speak of our Christian faith.

Again, I emphasise the need for political correctness which may seem, at first sight, an excuse not to speak of our faith. That would be wrong because there is still a right to free speech but how that is done without inferring that others are wrong or in faiths other than Christianity, are not tolerated or that anything a Christian says makes that inference, would be quite wrong for the very best reasons. There is a real hope – at least for me – that people I know will recognise the difference between living a 'good' life, regularly attending church services or activities and of a life that is wholly committed to the Lord Jesus.

I think that we have to answer the question, 'Are we active or passive Christians?' Passivity may be an excuse not to speak of our faith where circumstances would permit such a conversation. However, to be an active Christian does not mean that we can speak or preach about Jesus at any time or in any place. That would be a real put-off by anyone who would want to avoid us! But it does infer that we are unashamed of our faith and ready to give a reason for the hope we have and in what we believe and know.

In today's climate, it would be wrong if, in speaking of our faith, we offend anyone whether intended or not. An inference that another faith or religion is wrong or, indeed, that someone who professes not to have any faith or religion at all, that we denounce anything other than Christianity, is quite out of the question and could lead to public criticism or even legal action. The bible actually says 'love your enemies'… wow, is that possible?

Thus, a Christian needs to be sensitive and certainly to be understanding and be a good listener. My references in these chapters when making the point, referring back to my horrific dream which still haunts me, 'You never told me' are not actually about speaking primarily but about *living* the Christian life ie. that actions speak louder than words.

So let us be careful; let us be mindful of others' opinions and life-styles. Let us as Christians not be confrontational but living examples of what we believe. It is quite remarkable that many non-Christians will ask 'Why are you helping?'; 'Why are you so caring?' Yes, we need to have a ready answer to such questions but we need to be careful and even slow to immediately touch on our faith. Yes, we ought to be ready to do so when the right time and occasion demands it. Of course, we have to be living a life which doesn't contradict our belief and trust in Jesus.

It is challenging to read in Matthew's Gospel the illustration used by Jesus about talents. Three illustrations of gifts from Him to be used wisely. When they returned to the master, two did use the talents given but one failed to use his talent. He hid it! Surely, if we who are called Christians used the gifts the Lord has given us… use them. Being shy of our Christian life, being afraid to be His witness, being neglectful of helping others whatever their circumstances does not have any commendation from the Lord Jesus. Are we shy? Or are we afraid?

And a final word before you read on – when on a course at Sandhurst, my tutor was one of Britain's high ranking Army officers who, midst other very helpful instructions, simply said, 'Robin, only he who serves is qualified to lead.' To me this was supreme advice and in the Christian context if we are willing to, and actually do, serve others we have the opening and privilege to lead others to faith in the Lord Jesus. After all, as Christians we are servants!

Speaking with men… and sometime ladies, one of the big objections about Christianity is that it is out of date! I will discuss this later but the problem seems to be endemic that Christians are happy to use nineteenth-century language (thee, thou, vouchsafe etc.) and not recognise that modern language must surely not be optional but essential! Christian belief is up-to-date, is topical and certainly not of the nineteenth century!

Chapter 1

The dream

In 1968, in Memphis, Tennessee, Martin Luther-King stood in the street amongst an unruly crowd and some supporters; he knew that his popularity was not universal in America but he was a determined man... in two ways - determined with his strong convictions and determined in his hopes and dreams.

He knew the media was there as he spoke and in a sense, he hoped that his message to a few was to be broadcast to thousands. He didn't have a pulpit but, surrounded by a large crowd, he, on a small podium, began with a loud but quivering voice, 'I have a dream...'

What he was about to proclaim was largely drowned out by opposing screams for they knew his message; it wasn't new and it wasn't popular. Perhaps to many in the large crowd he was a distant figure and while many there would probably have agreed with his speech, an even larger crowd tried to shout him down. He had only started his shouting speech before others tried to shout and howl hoping to drown what he was saying. Sadly, and shockingly, he was assassinated.

Martin Luther King was leading a spreading view by many but not yet the majority; he was strongly against discrimination and his dream was that, one day, Americans would see discrimination as harmful, hurtful, vile, not right and ungodly. And not just for the black community but a message for all who believed in fair play and equality. He had hardly begun his well-prepared oration when the shot rang out! This great messenger and communicator was assassinated but his message continued through other voices; his life-long dream was for a truly united State of America. Perhaps his dream extended beyond America and spread to Africa, the Far East and indeed, to all civilised countries. And though he was unable to articulate his message to a divided nation he also had a dream that – one day – his beloved country might recognise its cruelty to those who were on the wrong side of discrimination. It was, of course, a message to us and all civilised countries.

So it was that Nelson Mandela in South Africa was also moved to speak out! After twenty-seven years' incarceration, his message reached those who had the power, and later the will, to cease the evil discrimination which many national leaders despised and to cease the feeling that South Africa was ostracised in trade, sport, tourism and so on. As it happened - because we were both officials in the Order of St John - I sat with Nelson Mandela in St James' Palace, London when we were both knighted within the Order.

Nelson was a godly man; his gentle, persuasive voice expressed no hatred of his former oppressors and he mentioned no regrets concerning his treatment but, following our long discussion, he delightfully summed it up: 'Robin, my dream came true and our loving God is now honoured by so many as we walk forward in His way on an equal footing.' Yet he was a sad man having to recognise that his views on discrimination were not popular with everyone and his sadness was underlined by the feeling that even Christian churches were not giving a wholehearted priority in their stance and preaching about the biblical teaching that discrimination is not only wrong at ground level but the message from God in the bible is for all people.

Interestingly, at a dinner in Atlanta, USA, during the Olympic Games committee meetings, I spent time with the now late Archbishop Tutu, also from South Africa. We talked about Nelson Mandela – they were naturally good friends. The Archbishop concluded our long conversation by summing up the South Africa changes with these simple words which I gladly memorised: 'Robin, our loving and faithful God, understands and we have to take on the burden of responsibility; in our walk with God we have not only the responsibility but also the obligation – and I say this reverently – to entrust to Him the ultimate answer because it is through Him with our prayer support, that things will eventually change. Robin, we have to pray, just pray, there must be much prayer and continued prayer. I am convinced that our loving Father in Heaven fully understands and will one day conquer the opposition. The dream continues!' What a long and lasting conversation that was!

I could mention others who had similar dreams such as Corrie ten Boom and Richard Wermbrandt who suffered for their beliefs *but* there was one massive advantage – all these dreamers had strong Christian faith which, sadly, many who dare to speak about it fail to live it out !It should be said that

21

for many Christians, it was a painful experience such as that of Dietrich Bonhoeffer whose dream was to see the renewal in Germany of Christian belief and full equality which had been squeezed out by pro-nazi propaganda, but who was murdered in a Concentration Camp before the dream was fulfilled. Underlying their efforts was complete reliance on God and their understanding that 'if God is for us, then who can stand against us?'

I fully recognise that I can, in no way, be counted amongst the great dreamers but I do have the same faith, albeit sometimes faltering and shy, but I also have had a dream! I don't have the same audiences as those I mentioned, nor the proclamation of the media either 'for' or 'against'. But let me outline my dream, almost a nightmare, so that you, as you read on, will understand my position and mission to share it.

My dream:

It was a quiet night after an uneventful day so there was nothing to trigger off a dream. Yes, I was tired and thus went to sleep quite rapidly. However, my mind was at work and I dreamt that I had suddenly died. There seemed to be no fear but I was aware that a vast noisy crowd was around me; I was in the open-air with a heavy atmosphere; it was loud, I was amongst a noisy, angry crowd in an intimidating atmosphere and I was unable to reach, let alone pass through, the vast gates of heaven. The shouting crowd was molesting me; there were tugs and pulls to get their attention; the shouting grew in its intensity but I couldn't understand what was being yelled. In my attempts to push through the crowd, it became clear what was in the din. Some were shouting so loudly that I felt

I was being deafened, 'You never told me,' 'You never told me'; others pushed their faces into mine and accused me more personally, 'You never told me'; 'You never told me'. I was being manhandled, buffeted by angry people like revisiting many of the demonstrations which I had policed in my long career.

The gates of Heaven were getting further away and I was on the point of tears and breaking down when an unidentified man and his wife calmly whispered in the uproar, 'You never told us about the love of Jesus. Why didn't you tell us? You lived with us, you worked with us, you befriended us but you never told us...'

With a sudden jolt, with screaming in my ears, I woke up – shaken to the core! With a shock! I sat up, sweating and horrified. It was real and more than a dream. It was so true... many, many people could rightfully accuse me of failing to tell them of the Lord Jesus.

As I regained full consciousness, I got out of bed, walked around in the darkness of night realising that this dream was far too real, so accurate, but what to do now? Do I go to every house in the neighbourhood, knock on the door and give them the Gospel? Do I bore everyone at the golf club with talk of salvation? Do I witness at the Royal British Legion? a tirade of thoughts came through my mind... yes, the dream was more than a nightmare and I began to realise that the experience was more than a nightmare because it was actually true to life. I wasn't a great missionary; I wasn't someone who naturally spoke of faith in the Lord Jesus... how many people I had known who had now passed into eternity not knowing or experiencing the love of Christ in their lives? Yes, as in the dream, so many people could rightly shout, 'You never told me!'

As the night wore on and daylight began to penetrate, so rationality and reason slowly flowed into my thoughts. It was wrong to start trying to reach people without first seeking the right way from God Himself. I was at a clear junction in my life. Surely, now I had to translate all I had dreamt into prayer, recognising my own unworthiness and maybe reticence but realising too that something had to change. Paul's words in the bible came to mind very quickly - 'by all possible means some might be saved' (1 Corinthians 9.22) and then Jesus' words to His disciples 'go and make disciples of all nations' (Matthew 28.19) and gradually understanding that that verse was prefaced by Jesus 'all authority in heaven and earth has been given to Me'.

So my first resolve in response to the dream should have been regular and constant prayer, preparation, seeking His way, allowing the Holy Spirit to inspire and strengthen, to give wisdom and discernment with a real intention to be more ready and available to share the Gospel. However, in my foolish way, I tried to forget the dream saying, quite literally, to myself, 'it was only a dream' but, and it is a big but, I could not shake it off such that I had to recognise there was much truth in what I had dreamt – in fact, it was a nightmare! I had to take the dream seriously and improve my poor witness realising that I should learn from it and, maybe, help others to learn from it.

Dreams may not be the way God speaks to us all though in Scripture there are dreams which have been very real in their interpretation. For example, Joseph -wrongly imprisoned - was inspired to interpret the meaning of simultaneous dreams which had been received by fellow prisoners and, interestingly,

Joseph said to the two men, 'Do not interpretations belong to God?' (Genesis 40.8). Joseph was then inspired to take up courage and then tell the men their fate when explaining the dreams' meanings.

Similarly, Daniel was used by God to interpret the dream of King Nebuchadnezzar which to him was not exactly good news! (Daniel 2.1 and 17 et seq.) There are numerous instances of dreams in Genesis, Deuteronomy, Judges, Samuel, Isaiah and Jeremiah. Even in the New Testament, Joseph, when he learned of Mary's pregnancy, felt he should quietly divorce his wife but – and I quote – 'the Lord appeared to him in a dream and explained that the baby she had conceived was from the Holy Spirit'. Then, after the birth of Jesus, three Magi visited Him in the manger but were warned in a dream not to return to the scheming King Herod so they altered their route home. And then the link with Old and New Testaments; Joel 2.28, speaking of the last days states, inter alia, that 'old men will dream dreams' and then, quoting that Scripture in Acts 2. 17, 'in the last days God says He will pour out His Spirit on all people... and your old men will dream dreams.'

I fully accept that biblically, dreams were nearly always interpreted or explained. With that in mind, I have sought, in prayer, to understand what my dramatic dream was actually meaning in real life. I have concluded that it was not limited simply to telling people about the Lord Jesus and, thereby, explaining the way of salvation. I believe the dream was a much bigger challenge than that and therefore the wider call is to live a life which is expected of a born again Christian which includes seeking to help the family, in its widest context; seeking to help neighbours and friends in any way possible;

visiting the sick either at home or in hospital or nursing homes; spending time with the aged and infirm, the many who rarely leave home; and those living alone (especially when a widow or widower have their only family many miles away who were rarely able to visit). Maybe, do the shopping, giving a lift in the car, helping in a garden, mowing a lawn, cutting hedges etc. There really is no limit to what can be done by those of us who love the Lord which means an outward-looking life; telling people about the Lord Jesus may therefore be an eventual opportunity rather than immediacy!

I am reminded of the Parable of the Sower and the Seed which Jesus related. Not everyone to whom we witness will respond by turning to Christ; the Devil will intervene and take away the Word from hearts; others will hear the Word but because of the stony ground [perhaps a hard-heart against 'religion' or 'I'm alright as I am'] the Word cannot take root even after receiving it happily; others will hear the Word but because of their busy lives, again, there would be no root for it because of life's worries, riches and pleasures. Then, wonderfully, there will be those to whom we witness with the Word of God who will receive it, take hold of it and have changed lives and they, themselves, become witnesses and share the Word.

However, for me the dream was a frightening nightmare which daunted me for a long while because it was a means of pulling me up and actually underlying a 'truism'. I am sure that there are far too many people who I have met, with whom I have worked, neighbours in the several places I have lived and, of course, family members and many, many others to whom I didn't speak of the Lord Jesus. I have never wanted to be intrusive but that is no defence if I was too shy or not looking for the right opportunity to share my faith.

Perhaps there should not be too much reliance on today's dreams however - realistic though they may be - but having said that, we have a 'direct line' to God in prayer. I am sure that I am not too far out of line to say that if we have had a realistic dream, we should take this to God in prayer asking Him if it has a practical meaning. If so, we have a high privilege… or perhaps an obligation… to be true witnesses of the Lord Jesus.

Wherever we are, even if it is merely occasional, means we are not keeping in step with God and His leading in life. It may be worse if it is just on Sundays at church when the oft repeated prayers from a book or from the Pastor or leader in a non conformist church where the prayers are not personal or a reference to specific needs in our life. Perhaps a personal confession here is pertinent; my early days in the police service were hard work – much learning from books and on the job itself which meant continual shifts and sometimes too little sleep as a result of night duty and then court appearances morning and afternoon. Sadly, it meant that my time of prayer and bible reading at the start of the day was now a problem; it took second place and I believe it affected quite seriously my witness on and off duty.

In my second year on the beat, two friends including my brother in law, John Balchin, and I went to the Keswick Convention and camped by Derwentwater. It was a great 'holiday,' much bible teaching, meeting other Christians and a real sense of renewal. Offered by one of the speakers was to join 'The League of the Morning Watch' whereby participants promised under God two things – [i] every morning at least 15 minutes of bible reading and prayer and [ii] concern for others who don't know the Lord Jesus. I made this commitment along with others but directly to the Lord and recognised that I would have to rely wholly on Him when I resumed policing however 'inconvenient' or difficult it would be with awkward duties.

Yes, there were occasions when as constables we were ordered out of bed in the Section House (where single constables were housed) in emergencies to report immediately for duty but generally speaking it now made the difference when on Early Turn (parading at 5.45am) to get up that much earlier to read scripture and pray before reporting for duty. It was the beginning of a lifelong habit which still holds in retirement to spend time at the start of the day with our Father... now, gladly, much longer than that original promise of fifteen minutes.

Prayer, of course, is not a one-off occasion because as we walk with the Holy Spirit we can commune with God constantly in our everyday life and especially, bearing in mind my 'nightmare' of 'you never told me,' when we are seeking to help others and be aware of needs in the community all of which may give us the privilege of sharing our faith.

Paul's letter to the Romans is such a 'handbook' for Christians, perhaps especially Chapter 12 of this book *Life in Eternity* which is really a summary of the previous chapters. "I urge you, in view of God's mercy, to offer your bodies as living sacrifices, holy and pleasing to God. Do not conform to the pattern of this world but be transformed by the renewing of your mind. Then you will be able to test and approve what God's will is – His good, pleasing and perfect will.' Paul continues with that theme and in verses 11 to 13, a definite instruction 'Never be lacking in zeal, keep your spiritual fervour, serving the Lord.

Be joyful in hope, patient in affliction, *faithful in prayer.* Yes, this is about being with God's people but non-Christians will, I'm sure, recognise the difference and other snippets are also helpful 'bless those who persecute you; rejoice with those who rejoice, mourn with those who mourn; live at peace with everyone; feed your enemy if he is hungry or thirsty… overcome evil with good.'

So how can that accusation of never telling, or being a Christian witness, be answered?

'Here I am. Send me,' are words that come readily to mind (Isaiah 6.8) as I write; they are a stark reminder that I must not, and should not, keep my faith to myself. As Christians, we should be available always in His service, ready for any opportunity to show God's love wherever we are. I have heard it too often 'I like to keep my faith private' or 'This is my business; people don't want me to preach to them.'

Perhaps the following chapters will enable us to review our Christian stance and motivation and as I try to remember the song which included the words, 'Others, Lord, yes others; Let this my motto be.' I think these verses from Paul's letter to the Philippian Church is my motivation – 'Each of us (as Christians) should look not only to your own interests *but also to the interests of others.'* Philippians 2.4 and 'it is God Who works in you to will and to act according to His good purposes' Philippians 2.13.

One further word here is, I believe, essential. How many of our churches – of whatever denomination – do actually seek to save 'the lost'? I guess, and I think quite rightly, that if every service - morning and or evening - consisted of what many would call a Gospel service, that would be missing the mark since the pulpit should be used to teach the congregation from Scripture but I have to wonder if the Sunday service is geared only to Christian believers? Surely, if there is a regular congregation at the service, yes, there should be teaching from the Bible and application of that teaching into believers' lives but also a recognition that it is probable that not everyone in the pew or in the chairs has been born again by the Spirit of God! Surely ministers or others leading the services or preaching, should recognise that even despite a regular congregation, some – maybe be only one or two – may have never been converted! That would be disastrous on the day of judgement!

Reflection: Have you had a dream or a nudge from God about your prayer life? You may feel powerless but that is not a weakness; it is a reminder that God is saying, 'I am always with you' and therefore able to reach you and use you to reach others. I call to mind the prayer of Paul in 1 Corinthians 9.22 'that by all possible means some might be saved.' Maybe through you and me!

It is possible, surely, to turn dreams into reality. When I reflect on my life and though I treasure my faith, and I treasure the times and many churches in which I have worshipped or had the privilege of preaching, and am deeply sad that comparatively few ladies, men and young people have come to a real faith in the Lord Jesus. I am sad, too, that some of those churches are not what I call 'outreach churches.' Satisfied that the ritual of weekly morning – and even evening services – is helping the regular attendees but rarely with any challenge about whole-hearted commitment and, even more sadly, without any form of outreach to the village or surrounding town. Some churches don't have a Prayer Meeting which might include praying earnestly for our wider family, neighbours, colleagues, school-teacher... the list could go on. 'Why?' I say – 'do we have little or no concern for those who have no faith?'

How many of our friends, neighbours, colleagues, those with whom we play sport, people we meet when out at the shops... indeed dozens of people who could make the accusation that I had in my dream could shout 'you never told me!'

I want to say something else about my beloved son Steve. Before his funeral at Manchester Cathedral, there was an hour's 'celebration' of his life in his office alongside all his colleagues. His boss, the Detective Inspector read a portion of Scripture and said 'this is our opportunity to emphasise the importance of our Steve in the office and in our work. I'll ask all of you who would like to say something in respect of Steve, please do so but I would like to be first! I knew of Steve's high reputation as an officer when he arrived here and I knew that he was a Christian. I thought, 'Oh dear, how is he going to fit in?' The Inspector then said, 'Steve's faith and his expertise changed my life! I was not a church-attender but I was so moved by Steve – his expertise, his good listening skills and his Christian faith, I realised that this was what was missing in my life. Steve prayed with me privately and I received Jesus into my life.' Others of Steve's colleagues, police women and male officers, said things similarly to that of 'the boss' and one young man, new to the Squad finished the occasion by saying, 'I came here shy of my new-found faith. How would I be treated? Then Steve took hold of me, we prayed together and he said 'we don't preach here but just do the best job we can and that is our witness.'

At his funeral, I was asked by dear Lesley, his widow and our daughter-in-law, to welcome the hundreds in the Cathedral. A daunting task but I concluded by saying, 'This morning is not 'Goodbye Steve' but for us as Christians we simply say, 'See you later!' That caused quite a stir in the Press but you can read of that in another book of mine *Father, Forgive*.

Chapter 2

Setting the scene

Now why should my dream be so startling, almost haunting, so that I am compelled to respond? I was converted undramatically at a Boy Crusader Camp at Studland Bay, Dorset in my teen-age years and although my lovely parents, at that time, were not Christians, my elder sister, Cherry, had at the age of thirteen, been told she ought to be confirmed but she hadn't been christened! So one dramatic week-end she was christened – and the next Sunday she was confirmed! That week, too, my sister Wendy was christened and God parents had been summoned to the service and then it was realised that I, too, ought to be christened so two of my parents' friends (they were Jewish and he a chiropodist in Bond Street, London) were invited and made to be my God-Parents! Never once did they talk to me about the Christian faith!

Cherry at college saw the difference that mere attendance at church regularly did not translate into her a personal faith unless she recognised her position, confessed her sin realising that the Lord Jesus had died for her (and the world), that she could be forgiven and ask the Lord to come into her life. A radical new start and she had the encouragement of active Christians on the staff and with some fellow students. So Cherry arrived home during a College vacation and announced that she had been converted and was now a Christian!

My other sister (Wendy) and I sat in silence as the discussion went on but it was soon evident that Cherry was different in a positive way. Dad sat silent but Mother said, 'Well, we're all Christians, aren't we?' Difficult to explain now though I suppose very roughly Cherry had changed and she was much more helpful in the house, wanted to share her new found faith and wanted to talk about it. Neither Wendy nor I were Christians at the time though we continued at church but with Cherry's encouragement, Wendy became a Christian at an evangelistic rally in Redhill, Surrey under the ministry of Tom Rees of Hildenborough fame and I was converted at the Crusader camp at Studland Bay, Dorset some time after that, as explained above.

Mum and Dad were wonderfully converted late in life but the point of me explaining this family detail is that Cherry couldn't contain herself and wanted to share her experience with others. She knew now that she had a reason for the faith that she now had [1 Peter 3.15] and not only was there a real desire to share it with others but, as she discovered, there is an obligation for all Christians to be ambassadors, representing Christ wherever we are [2 Corinthians 5.20] and He making His appeal through us.

When Cherry finished her Physical Training, she was appointed P.E. Teacher in Guildford which meant that she lived at home and, in fact, started a Bible Study Group at our house in Hooley, Surrey on a Monday evening to which upwards of 30 people came including the local vicar from Chipstead! And what a terrific group that became with friends from different denominations from far and wide joining in the helpful discussions.

The night before I joined the Metropolitan Police, I went with Cherry, after the Evening Service at church, to meet a fellow Gym Teacher at her home in Purley and clear Christian, Olive Perrett, whose husband, Ron, was a police officer in Croydon. The three of us listened to Ron about the Training School and the challenges to be faced and, afterwards, when on the beat. At the end of the evening we prayed together, and as Cherry and I walked down the front garden path, Ron called out, 'Robin, nail your colours to the mast.' That took a bit of understanding but he meant, don't keep your faith a secret.

I wasn't immediately wholly sure about that but next morning, I arrived at the Police Training School along with another fifteen young men and four ladies. We were all unknown to each other, rather shy but all in the same boat… naïve perhaps and wondering how tough and different the thirteen weeks' training would be. We were all fitted out with uniforms which had to be pressed and boots which had to be 'bulled' and an Instruction Book from which we had to learn by heart the first four paragraphs by next morning! Very late that night I went to my small cubicle in the Dormitory, quite tired, and quickly prepared for bed and knelt by the bed to pray as was my normal custom. Within moments, my new colleague, who was next door, banged open my door and, in a loud voice, yelled 'What the hell do you think you're doing. Your feet are in my cubicle!' Whoops! The room space was minimal and I had not noticed that the plywood partition between 'rooms' had a six inch gap from the floor; I was praying with my feet in his space!

I didn't need to nail my colours to the mast after that – it was done next morning by my new 'friend' who explained to the class what the yelling was last night. Game, set and match! I have to say that I wasn't given too hard a time though the training Sergeants and Inspectors soon cottoned on and frequently made reference to my Christian faith. It is not an exaggeration to say that from Training School to my first posting and thereafter wherever I served, my Christian stance went before me.

Though I soon joined the Christian Police Association – the National HQ was within half a mile of the Training School and I introduced myself there while still in training. – I have to say that as a young, probably naïve, believer, I found witnessing and talking about my faith, was never easy. However , there was much joy too when sometimes, a colleague would be interested and, even more occasionally, come to faith in Christ. On all Promotion Boards, as I progressed through the ranks, I came to expect that one of the Board members would ask about my faith in terms such as 'what's it like to be a Christian in the station?' or 'how does it affect your work' or 'can you help speaking about it in the station or to people you meet, prisoners etc.' And the regular ending to that kind of remark 'Doesn't being a Christian hinder your actions as an officer?'

I often wondered why such questions were necessary; after all, I had passed the appropriate examinations and been recommended by senior officers to attend a Promotion Board. I was thoughtful, careful and honest in my responses because my first priority was to be an effective police officer. Wonderfully, the initial shyness disappeared; my prayer life became more effective at any time of the day or night and wherever I was. I cannot dare say that my faith made me a better police officer than I might have been but I am certain that it made Robin Oake, in whatever rank or position, a better man than I would have been without my faith. Of course, I had a wonderful and loving wife – having married Chris. soon after my invitation to serve in New Scotland Yard as a mere young constable with 3 years service, who prayed for me and supported me as I worked, despite having to be away from home for much of the time and, later, she bringing up three children.

With that rather long outline, I am still haunted and feeling guilty about the number of times I could have spoken about the Lord Jesus but didn't! I am staggered that so many, many colleagues and neighbours, friends, those with whom I had to deal in policing – where does it end? - who could now point the finger at me and bellow, 'You never told me!' I was really amazed, some years later, on a Promotion Board to Chief Inspector, the Chairman, Commander Pennington, welcomed me, asked me to sit down and simply said without any embarrassment, 'Mr Oake, I too have become a Christian since we last met and I look forward sometime to spend time with you about my new faith.' Wow, what a start to the Promotion Board questions!

So I am sure it is worth looking at life and seeing where we can be clear in our testimony and actually see or seek the opportunities to telling people of Jesus. Having said that, it is also true that Christians may lose their first love of Christ and, thereby, lose their will and intention to share their faith with others. Yes, still attend church services and activities but introverted about their faith!

Reflection: Is your personal life strengthened daily by prayer at home or wherever you are? Is God prompting you to be more active in your witness?

Why not specifically ask God to lead you this week to help someone who is in need and that by such a kind act, that you may have the opportunity to speak about your faith?

There is no encouragement for a dormant Christian!

So before you read on, I think it would be a real help to thoroughly examine where we stand as a Christian, what it is that *we* believe so that when the opportunity eventually comes to answer queries about the Christian faith, we can be confidently sure of our ground. How about starting with what is known as the Apostles Creed?

'I believe in God, the Father almighty, creator of heaven and earth. I believe in Jesus Christ, His only Son, our Lord, Who was conceived by the Holy Spirit, born of the virgin Mary, suffered under Pontius Pilate, was crucified, died and was buried; He descended to the dead. On the third day, He rose again; He ascended into heaven; He is seated at the right hand of the Father and He will come to judge the living and the dead. I believe in the Holy Spirit, the holy catholic church, the communion of saints, the resurrection of the body and the life everlasting'

This is a sure foundation for Christian believers for whatever denomination to which we are accustomed or wherever we worship.

Chapter 3

Evangelism and the evangelist

In a real and practical sense, what you will read from here on is about evangelism and, I deliberately put this first, ahead of what is to follow, the calling of an evangelist. What a great gift from God – to be a full-time evangelist. However, the evangelist, speaking, say, in a church, or at a large rally in a town, or at a University – wherever – relies totally on you and me as Christian believers who have the responsibility to invite, in whatever way possible, non-Christians to come and hear the evangelist! To hear the Gospel.

Surely - and I really have to underline this - principally, a local church has a huge responsibility not only to strengthen its congregation in the Christian faith but it also has a biblical obligation to evangelise! If we truly believe that we are born again, have had new life in Christ, not only is there the privilege to reach out but also to ensure that we as Christians are willing witnesses. Within the fellowship there ought to be regular times of prayer together for the village 'outside,' the town nearby and members of our family and friends.

Does our church have a regular and insistent regular prayer meeting? Does our local church train its people in evangelism, in witness and in sharing the good news of the Gospel? It is most surely a sad situation if the church is simply and only a meeting place on Sundays for regular attenders. Yes, they are there for fellowship and worship but if there is no urgency for evangelism, no concern that the majority of their friends and or local villagers; our neglect is the misfortune of non-Christians! Are we going to face the accusation I had in my dream 'You never told me!?' Apart from that, a fulfilled Christian life is sharing one's faith, having the real joy of introducing someone to faith in Christ. '*Oh no,*' I heard someone say; '*I keep my faith private - to myself.*'

If we are part of a church fellowship, we have not only the privilege of meeting and sharing with fellow believers but also, there should surely be the added dimension of sharing such friendship with others. We might think that we are too shy, maybe embarrassed, to talk about our faith…. but we don't share it on our own. I think of several verses in Scripture which underline - firstly, that we share our faith in the strength which God supplies – viz. 'He is able to do immeasurably more than we ask or imagine according to the power that is at work within us (Ephesians 3.20). And Paul's letter to Timothy – 'Do not be ashamed to testify about our Lord….(2 Tim.1.8). Then, secondly, there are those incredible words in 1 Peter.2.9 'You are a chosen people - a chosen person – belonging to God that you may declare (yes, you may declare!) the praises of Him Who called you out of darkness into His wonderful light.' And again, in 1 Peter 3.15 'In your heart, set apart Christ as Lord and always be prepared to give an answer to everyone who asks you to give the reason for the hope that you have.' Perhaps the most telling of Jesus's teaching is in Matthew 14-30... the parable of talents. I have mentioned this before but it needs to be doubly emphasised! Talents given to three people two of whom used those talents to gain more for the Master but the one who hid his talent was condemned because he did nothing with it! If we have a living Christian faith it surely is not just for our own good but to be shared with others too!

How about us as Christians? We have been given so much to be used in His service and not be hidden through our shyness, lack of concern for others, fear of witnessing of our faith; failing to invite others to meet the Lord Jesus. This, I say with regret, is to our shame and, worse, failing to share with non Christians the salvation offered to all. God so loved the world... we, as Christians, are the advertisement!

Let non-Christians recognise the difference which our true faith makes in life; Jesus said of Christians 'You are the light of the world; let your light shine before others that they may see your good deeds and praise your Father Who is in heaven.'(Matthew 5.14-16). Does Jesus abhor any who are ashamed? I doubt that but His expectation, surely, is that we share our faith – after all, we are His witnesses. I guess that most church attenders are not actually ashamed of their faith in Jesus but feel unable to freely speak of their faith in Him. Is it shyness, is it that we are embarrassed? We ought to remember that He, by His Spirit, is IN US WHO BELIEVE so our witness is not only seen in the way we live but in our conversations and our concern for others.

Much should be made of Missionaries Societies and their role in our world today. Personally, I think that they have too low a profile for the fantastic work that they undertake. A list of such 'societies' would take a sizeable book but where there is a need at home or abroad, many Christians have recognised it and founded a missionary society. Indeed, the Christian Police Association, founded in the late nineteenth century, was initiated by Miss Catherine Gurney because of a general lack of respect for police. Started initially of what was called the International Christian Police Association Forces, it encouraged and emboldened Christian officers and their families. Now known as CPA, it is well known not only in the British Isles but also in North America, the Far East, on the European continent and so on.

My concern is that we who have a Christian faith do not meet the need – generally speaking, of our fellow men, women and families. So in addition to CPA, very many other needs are met by other missionary societies specific to particular circumstances so my general criticism of our inability to reach the general public certainly does not encroach on or include the many, many missionary associations in Britain and elsewhere who do so much good – often with little monetary reward – to openly profess and preach the Gospel.

Additionally, a grass-roots church fellowship ought to be able to seek help in personal evangelism so that gifted folk can be encouraged to speak and teach about evangelism. Does our local church have regular courses to teach and explain the purpose of evangelism? Does the church assist Christians who sincerely want to introduce friends to Christ and personal faith in Him but feel unable to do so? I guess it is easy to talk about our favourite soccer team, their latest score at 'home' or away; to talk about cricket and especially this new form of cricket called The Hundred. We find it easy to pass the time of day 'Good morning,' 'Good Evening' etc. We easily talk about the shops, the prices; we talk about the price of fuel for our car and so on yet, and I say this very reluctantly, we fail to easily talk about our faith! I am not saying – God forbid – that every time we meet neighbours, friends, colleagues etc. we talk about our faith and that alone; I doubt that they would welcome that and may even try to avoid us! But what I am trying to say is that in our normal day to day conversations about things of interest, we ought also to pray that at some time we should be ready to talk about our Christian faith and the difference it makes to us and for us. Obviously, what we don't want is for neighbours and friends to say to themselves as they see us the street, 'Whoops, another sermon' or 'Come on, let's go another way.' We don't want people to have to avoid us in case we nobble them to become Christians. What I am saying is 'Be prepared in our friendships – and indeed with others we don't really know – to share our faith as the opportunities afford.' Sometimes, it is just being a practical help one way or another which eventually gives the clear opportunity to speak about our Christian faith.

What would be the point of an invited evangelist to come either for a week or so, even longer, or for an evening Rally, if the only people there to listen were already born-again believers or just regular church attenders? Much of what is being said in the following chapters is about witness and evangelism – often one to one – but the Evangelist relies not only on the love of God and the Holy Spirit's power but on you and me inviting non Christians to hear the Gospel – and what we believe.

My early days as a young Christian were in the era of Billy

Graham and the mammoth meetings held throughout the world but, in my case, in London initially at Harringay Arena, and later in Earls Court; then further afield in Liverpool at Anfield Football Stadium. Yes, there were crowds, large crowds, but Billy would not have been used by God in the way he was if only Christian folk were in the audience. He and his team relied on ordinary people like you and me to invite non Christians to the rallies to hear the Gospel. Similarly, the local 'church' – you and me – have a responsibility one way or another to share our faith. It may not primarily be to speak the Gospel but that may follow if we show our concern for neighbours and, indeed family, but helping, say in shopping for them; helping in the garden, giving them a lift in the car – there are so many ways in which we can show our care for others which may, in time, also be the avenue to speak of our faith which could challenge others to believe.

My awful dream you remember had this dreadful accusation 'You never told me…' which might also mean 'you never showed any concern for me… you went to church but never invited me… I knew there was something different about you but you never explained it to me…'

My good friend Roger Carswell who I mentioned before– a great evangelist used by God in so many ways - is wholly reliant on local churches, Christian Unions in Universities etc. doing their work with advertising Roger's meetings, reliant on people like you and me personally inviting and taking friends, colleagues, neighbours – anyone – to attend the meetings to hear the Gospel through Roger. In addition to speaking in churches, he is often working with University Christian Unions and it is the Christian students who do the ground-work in prayer and with invitations to meet with and hear Roger speaking. This, of course is the case with all full-time evangelists – we are needed to invite people to hear the Gospel – personally or through publicity.

I mention Roger but there are many, many other full-time evangelists whose delight is to speak to non- Christians and back-sliders so that God Himself can speak to empty hearts. I love the phrase in the Bible 'do the work of an evangelist'. Paul, in writing to Timothy his friend, urged him to keep his head in all situations *and* do the work of an evangelist (2 Timothy 4.5). Most of us are not called to be an evangelist in the same sense of Billy Graham or Roger – and indeed many, many others who stand up and preach the Gospel but their ministry is reliant on people like you and me living out our Christian belief in practical ways and taking the opportunity to invite those who we know and meet to hear God's messengers. That is 'doing the work of an evangelist'… practically, living for others to be an example of what it is to be a true Christian.

Having acclaimed the calling of an Evangelist, it surely is pertinent that ordained ministers, in any Christian denomination, or those who have the privilege of preaching either as church leaders or as an invited guest preacher, should be aware that they have an obligation, at the very least, to explain the Gospel. We who stand in pulpits must never assume that all who are sitting in pews or on chairs are already Christians. There is nothing meant here in a judgmental way, but at the end of their lives, how many who have been regular church-attenders are going say 'You never told me' or 'You never even challenged me'? As an instance, I attended church and Sunday School practically every week of my early years on earth and was ignorant of the need to be born again. I guess that could be repeated thousands and thousands of times!

Reflection: How much do I support the many evangelists who, week in and week out, at various venues, have the opportunity to preach the Gospel to unbelievers? They need prayer support and, all too often, financial support too. And their ministry is, surely, an example of what we should be and, dare I say it, praying that our church vicars, ministers, church leaders should be doing... the work of an evangelist as well as Christian teachers. What a privilege they have week in and week out to open Scripture to congregations but it is surely part of their calling to do the work of an evangelist!

The following chapters are about how we live for Christ amongst unbelievers because, ultimately, non Christians are our 'audience' and their response to the Gospel may well be how we live our lives, about our conversations, about our response to help needy people and so on...in that sense, doing the work of an evangelist. So here we go – looking and discussing the life we live amongst many unbelievers, I guess most of whom have no idea of the life they could have in Christ and, dare I say, until they meet us! Whoops!

The words of Francis of Assissi are especially appropriate, now turned into a hymn 'Make me a channel of Your peace' summed up, perhaps, in the chorus words, 'Master, grant that I may never seek so much to be consoled as to console, to be understood as to understand, to be loved as to love with all my soul.'

And as a reminder for all who have the privilege of preaching... Ephesians 4.11 'It was Jesus Who gave some to be apostles, some to be prophets, some to be evangelists and some to be pastors and teachers…' and the reason for this? 'to prepare God's people for works of service so that the body of Christ may be built up.' Not simply for Christians to be pew-fillers each Sunday, meeting, as it were, to attend 'the club' but for all of us to put into practice God's gifts in sharing the Gospel by practical witness always seeking ways to serve the Master and, in that, always looking for the opportunity to introduce a neighbour, a friend, others who we regularly meet, to faith in Christ.

Chapter 4

The family

As wife and husband, it is essential, obviously, that we love each other, spend time with each other and pray together. It amazes me when I see married couples who once walked arm in arm or hand in hand, never now doing so in public! Why has that intimacy disappeared? If we are to be judged by others about our Christian faith, surely one of the 'messages' that we should give is that we love each other and depend on each other. We are in a world where love seems to be too shallow, or where in some cultures, a wife – indeed any woman – is treated as second class. What a shop-window we have as Christians to exhibit true and lasting love, have a concern not only for our family but also for our neighbours, colleagues at work and others who we know. I think we need to exhibit to all who recognise us as Christian folk that we love each other however young, middle-aged or old we are – that we pray together, share the household chores together, garden together and be gracious to one another so that the peace of God's love is evident to visitors. These virtues are, of course, essential for our children to recognise as they grow up… examples for their own lives.

If there were to be a priority, then the family must come first. As Christian parents, we need to live a life which reflects our commitment to the Lord Jesus. Above all things, we need to regularly pray for our child or children that they may see in us something of that gracious living and loving whether it is in encouragement or reproof. At the earliest opportunity, we need to pray not only *for* our children but, maybe in the simplest way at first, *with* our children so that they grow up and mature and recognising not only the faith of parents but also understanding our commitment. Telling them about God's love and about the Lord Jesus should be as natural as having breakfast!

Now I recognise that family life is not always easy; that there are misunderstandings and disagreements and things get taken out of context. This means that there should also be forgiveness, times to really listen to each other and – as parents – be an example. Telling about Jesus and His love by parents who don't actually live that out is a real put-off. Fairness in reprimand is far better than yelling, 'You ought to know better!' Always look for a way of reconciliation.

We have to understand the pressures put on our children at school, at college or university, in the work place and, therefore be ready to hear of their problems and pray with them too. Encourage as much as possible without interference; sympathise rather than admonish. We had to face school discipline; we had to study alongside others who were brighter than us; we had to take taunts but I believe that that with which we grew up is now far worse in many situations so patience as parents is essential. After all, we are, primarily, their examples not only in how to cope with problems and difficulties but also how to put faith into action. We should always not only to be available to our children but also be understanding – or allow them to open up to us about the things, the temptations, the taunts, the unfairness of school life and even their own social life, helping them to choose their friends and so on.

How awful it would be, though, if at the end of it all, our children said to us, 'You never told me'; or 'Your actions spoke louder than your words'; that church going was a mere boring formality and not lived out at home. What a disaster!

Oh to have a church fellowship with many children and young people in attendance. Young mothers and babies; a decent Sunday School (or is that out of date?); a Young People's Fellowship where boy meets girl in the very best sense of that, learning together not only from biblical teaching but also learning how to put Christian faith into practice. Certainly my wife and I had that privilege before and during our first years of marriage in a lively and active church, which gave us confidence to live the Christian life without embarrassment or shyness.

How sad it is that there is a decline in church attendees; that young people see nothing for them in formal services and that it is not relevant in the 22nd Century. As parents, it is absolutely essential, difficult though it may be, to show that Christian faith *is* pertinent for every day living, that it is not old-fashioned and only for another generation! Surely, it is imperative that church services may not be judgemental (even change that name 'service?!'), missions, any outreach, be attractive in presentation, in its music and biblical preaching and teaching plus hearing personal testimonies.

To the minds of probably the majority of people, church and Christianity have no real meaning. Many live comfortable and satisfying lives… maybe with their families, with their leisure time and hobbies… and cannot see the pertinence of Christianity or, as they would probably call it, of religion. I wholly understand that but recognise also that the fault lies not with them but with us as Christians who have not made any impact of their lives. So the focus must be back on us as with our lively faith because we have not made any impact on the lives of neighbours, colleagues and friends.

Most of us have good friends and many relatives; as adults, we have, sadly and unfortunately, made little impact on our adult friends. Even if they think we are different with our own interests and only see us as 'religious' - maybe slightly strange. I also have to recognise that as adults and parents, many of our children with so many non Christian impacts on their lives with modern media and hand-held devices and other attractions, there are many, many sad Christian parents who despair about their non-Christian children. We as adults, happy in our Christian belief, in good company at church and its activities are probably very sad that our children are not understanding or even wanting, religion (as they would call it) in their lives.

Do they see in us the truth of the Gospel? Are we leading lives that attract them to Jesus or detract them? Paul wrote to Timothy (2 Timothy 1.1-5) about his grandmother and mother and how they gave their Christian example to Timothy. If our offspring don't see the real difference in our lives, rather than simply the fact that we regularly attend church services, then they will not see any relevance about the Christian faith. So a high priority in a Christian's life must be close family, and the wider members too, recognising that Christian faith makes a positive difference.

Chapter 5

The neighbourhood

Most of us live side by side with neighbours and, generally speaking, we probably get on well with them. But may be our contact with them is merely a cheery, 'Hello' or a wave as we walk or drive past them. Paul, in one of his letters to the churches, sums up all that needs to be said in this chapter, 'Each of us should please his neighbour for his good!' (Romans 15.2).

Neighbours are priority number two! It is easy for them to see that we regularly attend church services and activities so that there should be an evident difference in our lives to show why we are Christians. Some neighbours either keep themselves to themselves or like to keep us at arms length for no other reasons that they have their own friends or travel to relatives, have holidays at home or abroad etc. So they are not easily contacted. But, many people are lonely – shut in their home or flat or feeling very sad in a Nursing or Residential Home. There are many aged folk, some still with their husband or wife; some as widows or widowers. Maybe their family members are now living far away, even abroad and therefore are not often visited by them. If we know some like that, do we pray for them; do we visit and listen to them; do we share our faith with them?

I meet some who are living in poverty, just about on the bread-line. Yes there are a few 'food banks' but if anyone is housebound as well as poor, surely it is a Christian act to either shop for them or go to the food bank to sustain them. We need to spend time with such people to understand their real needs and the kind of food that they like and to which they look forward.

We could easily get it for them... even pay where necessary!

So let us look at the these situations. Friendly neighbours are an absolute boon; we can speak freely over the fence, or as we pass their front garden gate a simple 'Hello, how are you?' Nevertheless, they are friends who, at the end of the day, might well say to us, 'You never told me.' If in our neighbourness, we failed to ever speak about the Lord Jesus and the Gospel! Wow, how awful and, indeed, selfish! So how do we approach this situation? Firstly, regular prayer for them by name – parents, children, grandchildren. Secondly, meet them by calling in – best by telephoning first. The more we get to know them, the more we will know *about* them without being too inquisitive. They wouldn't take offence if we hear of a difficulty in their family and we promise to pray for them. No matter, anyway, what they think about prayer but it is a sure way of showing a genuine friendly interest. I read recently the following, which is so apt – 'Go often to the house of a friend and neighbour - for weeds choke the unused path!'

With such neighbours, there is usually much to share... in the garden, in the home, with the extended family, situations at work – these are matters which we may well have in common. In our prayers for them (do we?), seek to show understanding, sympathy where needed, encouragement and advice. I am very fortunate to have living a few doors away who is a tip-top computer man – which I certainly am not. It means that whenever I have a computer glitch, I call Richard in. What a guy, what a wife and family!

What about an annual 'get together' – i.e before Christmas or to celebrate the New Year? It's an opportunity for others in the road, lane, avenue or cul-de-sac to get to know each other. When my wife and I lived in the Isle of Man, our first Christmas was nine months after we went there and to get to know those in The Chase, we had an evening get-together with simple food and drink, chatting and one of us would speak for a few minutes about Christmas and its reason. We did this year after year as we got to know more people such that, before we moved back to England 22 years later; more than 60 neighbours and friends would come to this party, often saying that this is their annual highlight. None could say that they hadn't been told about the Lord Jesus and, as far as I know, any fear that they objected to the talk was never voiced. In fact, now, when we occasionally return to the Island, many will say how much they miss that Christmas evening!

Indeed, when we lived there, I was Chief Constable and I know that there were neighbours or people in the village who felt that they could not socialise with us because of my rank and job. I really hope it was not because Chris or I were aloof or that they felt we would not be interested in them. However, from my wife's perspective and my own, we kept our ear to the ground and, therefore, it was not unusual to hear of illness, injury, bereavement or some other crisis such that they would either ask us to come and visit them or we would take that opening to go and see how we could help. Often, we would not leave before we had prayed with them. That to us is absolutely natural.

So how about this? Our friends Jack and Hildegard lived just four doors away from our bungalow; Jack was diagnosed with a virulent form of cancer and his life was a nose-dive to eternity. We visited him regularly in Hospice and then, several days after his admission. the end of his life was signalled by the nursing staff - his final, sad, crisis. Hildegard telephoned and asked if we would come to his bedside with the family and make one last visit to read the bible and pray. Willingly, we went but Jack had been in a coma for three days. When we arrived in his room, I stood between the family and the silent Jack and read verses from John Chapter 14 and prayed for Jack, Hildegard and family - asking for God's wisdom and strength in the situation and praying especially for Jack. I was stunned when he, in that coma for three days, opened his eyes and firmly said aloud, 'Amen'. He then shut his eyes, stopped breathing and died! Had he heard? After all, it is said that 'hearing' is the last sense to go. Hildegard, who actually had a quiet relationship with God and was a close friend of Chris, was always grateful for that visit to Jack; she subsequently died... maybe they met in heaven!

Two of our golfing friends, Anne and Brian, had a son in the Royal Air Force, a pilot instructor in Nimrods - four-engined aircraft stationed in Scotland. Occasionally, as he and his 'pupils' flew over Port St Mary Golf Course, knowing that that was the day of competition there, the plane would waggle its wings in recognition. We were delighted to meet their son when he was on leave and visiting his parents. We had heard that he had then been posted abroad to assist in Afghanistan with aerial communication but, days later, soon after when the plane was being re-fuelled in flight, it caught fire which soon caused the Nimrod to explode, crash and which all on board were killed.

What a dreadful shock to the family. We heard of this on the radio and immediately went to see them to try and console them, comfort as much as we could and just be there in their grief. We were asked to pray with them while we were there – what a privilege – and, some time later, to attend his RAF Funeral at the base in Scotland. Yes, Anne and Brian were golfing friends as well as neighbours so they knew of our Christian faith but, dreadfully sad in their lives, it began a deeper friendship and times of sharing and prayer in their home.

While Chris and I were in Keswick for the Convention, we had a phone call from Denis, who was one of my staff when I was Superintendent in Moss Side, Manchester. We had the privilege of being invited to his wedding to a fellow officer, Denise. They had both found faith in Christ but the phone call was so sad – Denise had been taken ill into hospital where, soon after, she died prematurely. Despite the difference in our police ranks, we were good friends. So glad they rang – what a shock – but the funeral later was actually a real celebration of their faith. We are still in touch with Denis and his personal Christian faith.

I cite these examples of many where, I am sure because of our joint faith, Chris and I were always delighted with such contacts, and often, we were invited to help in crises in some way. Less dramatic circumstances could be cited but we are still in contact with Denis and other similar friends in police service. In every instance, there was always an opening to be with a colleague in whatever rank; a neighbour, a family member or a friend and share in their situation so we could put our arms around them as opportunity afforded, and pray. For all of us who don't live in isolation, there *are* opportunities to befriend, to share their problems and pray!

So, what about the neighbours either further away or not willing to be friendly? Surely they also need, at least, to hear about and consider God's love for them? There may well be opportunities to exhibit our faith if only we keep our ears to the ground. There may be illness; or a new-born baby; they may have been involved in a car accident; there may be a financial problem... the list could go on but such 'incidents' may enable us to show our care, get alongside and eventually be able to explain why; because it is a sure thing that they are thinking ... and will eventually ask us... why are you so interested in us? Why do you care? You hardly know us but here you are helping. That surely will, maybe after some time, enable us to give a reason for the hope that we have (1 Peter 3.15). Oh that they may never think or say, 'You never told me'.

Even if we are regular attenders at our local church, it may be that such opportunities are not yet being seen. Can we not suggest something more than coffee mornings – although they sometimes are an opening which gives grounds for speaking of our Saviour. Bible Study Groups? Young Wives Group? Men's Breakfasts? We need to pray for our church leaders that they and we may have open minds to what God is saying about 'outreach'. As Paul stated 'that by any means (or all possible means) some might be saved.' (1 Corinthians 9.22). Surely, as Christians, we must look for our opportunities and responsibilities.

Rural life, of course, is a far easier and identifiable mission field than inner cities. Villagers are often more friendly and give many more openings to us than, perhaps, compared with urban or city/town, banks of 'flats,' living on a barge, or simply inner-city or town dwellers. But please, we don't need to give up wherever we live. The majority of people amongst whom we live are not Christians; that is not necessarily because they have rejected the Gospel message but it is, perhaps, because they don't know what the Gospel is!

Sadly, *our* major problem is that we don't want to lose face or lose friendships; we're embarrassed to speak of the Lord Jesus and probably don't pray each day for openings, for caring, for listening to our village friends and acquaintances. How many of our neighbours are in our daily prayers? Do we even know their names?

That haunting song by Sidney Bertram Carter written in 1971 is about Jesus asking the crucial question…'When I needed a neighbour, were you there? And the creed and the colour and the name won't matter… were *you (was I?) there?* It continues 'I was hungry and thirsty – were you there? I was cold, I was naked – were you there? When I needed a shelter – were you there? Matthew 5.48 asks us to be perfect! Hardly possible in this life but we look to Jesus, the perfect Son of God and in His strength can be effective witnesses.

Will the needy people around us have cause to shout, 'You

never told me? Or, worse, we didn't know you were a Christian!' How embarrassing! And what would our Saviour think when He sees a need and asks 'Were you there - for Me - having pin-pointed the need for help?

This is the poem/hymn written by Sydney Carter (1915-2004) is so apt:

> *When I needed a neighbour, were you there?*
> *I was hungry and thirsty – were you there?*
> *I was cold, I was naked – were you there?*
> *When I needed a shelter - were you there?*
> *When I needed a healer – were you there?*
> *And the creed and the colour and the name won't matter,*
> *I'll be there.*

One other matter. I doubt many of us actually have enemies! I have already mentioned those who stood against Martin Luther King, against Nelson Mandela, against Deitrich Bonhoeffer and others and I hesitated to include what needs to be said about enemies in this chapter concerning neighbours but as Jesus never shied away from including those we find difficult in his teachings and what is expected from us, I feel I have to mention the subject. In Luke chapter 6 from verses 27 to 36, Jesus's word to us is very pertinent. Starkly He says, 'Love your enemies. Do good to those who hate you, bless those who curse you and pray for those who ill-treat you.' Continuing, Jesus says 'If someone strikes you on one cheek turn to him the other also. If someone steals your cloak, do not stop him from taking it. Give to everyone who asks you and if anyone takes what belongs to you, do not demand it back. Do to others as you would have them do to you.' Further on in the chapter, Jesus says, 'Forgive and you will be forgiven.' Wow, that's a different perspective!

So His teaching is not so much about enemies but about our attitude towards them. Yes, I am sure we all have those with whom it is difficult to get on; maybe, it is their behaviour which annoys us or the fact that they ignore us but this is surely an opportunity to pray for them and seek some way of showing our 'love' for them. I doubt we should call them enemies as such; because we shy away from these people, we have little opportunity of revealing our Christian way of life so, as Jesus says, 'pray for them.' Pray for an opening by which we can help, advise, be a good listener - simply showing that we care.

Reflection: Neighbours, by the very use of that word, see us, speak with us and share life with us.

Are we looking for, even hoping for, opportunities to share our concerns, to help where needed, be good listeners with the hope that one day we might share our faith and speak about the Lord Jesus?

Prayer: Lord, you know that I have neighbours in the same road and village, or in my town; Lord, please help me to keep my ear to the ground to listen out for any who are in need of some help or encouragement. Are there any, Lord, who could be invited for a meal, or need a garden tended; or repairs to their property but, perhaps, cannot afford a professional. Or, in their loneliness, they just need a friend to phone, to call in – to just be a listening ear. Yes, Lord, help me to recognise, as the hymn says, 'Others, Lord, yes others…let this my motto be'.

Chapter 6

Our colleagues at work

If we have retired from regular business or employment, we may now be regretting that we did very little to share our faith with former colleagues. Time cannot be rolled back but there are things which are possible in that situation. It may be possible, especially if we now pray for those with whom we worked or for whom we worked, that by praying for them individually and in general, asking our God to help them see the way of salvation; asking Him to introduce them to an active Christian. I am saying that we should never forget them! Prayer changes things!

It might be that former colleagues occasionally remember us and recognise that there was, in fact, something different about our attitude, our ability or the way we listened to them. They might remember the day when you stepped in to help or advise; when, maybe, they had a death or serious illness in their family and it gave opportunity to share the burden. It might have been a day when a colleague was having a financial problem and we silently stepped in to help with a loan or gift.

Then, what about organising a reunion? That's a God-given chance to meet colleagues again, see how they are faring in retirement; health matters will always be a topic! For example, years after I had left my first police station at St John's Wood and been promoted, moved Forces etc... a former colleague, Phill Williams, decided to round up any who had served in the years we were stationed there. Incredibly, he had done his homework and discovered the whereabouts of roughly 40 former officers; a date and hotel venue was arranged and included a visit to the police station and a formal dinner in the evening.

As my wife and I walked into the hotel, a fairly elderly man and his wife approached us and introduced themselves. Ray Smith was a senior constable when I arrived at St John's Wood and took a dislike to me by ridiculing my Christian faith. It hurt at the time but I never 'hit' back at his taunts. Here at the Reunion, I immediately recognised him and even remembered his name, thinking 'what on earth could he say to me? But, he immediately said, 'Robin, I owe you an enormous apology for the way I treated you at the station. I am truly sorry but you ought to know that soon after you left, my wife and I were converted; I left the police and after training went on the mission field in the Far East. We are home now on furlough but we were determined to come to this reunion to meet you again, to say that your witness was not in vain and not forgotten.' Seriously, wonders will never cease!

There is a challenge, however, for all who are still employed; in teaching; in administration; in the medical profession, in the building trade, as a professional sports person, in engineering, computer work... you name it, there are so many jobs - professional or artisan - each with their own enjoyments, challenges and satisfaction. How on earth do we get the balance between being good at our work, innovative where that is possible, conscientious so that we don't waste time in chatter and sharing our faith? I doubt there is a formula or a strict code of conduct except, maybe, that we should recognise why we are being employed and make that our true priority and objective. Having said that, if it is discovered that we are Christians, our colleagues will keep an eye on us, maybe not with any bad intent but simply because they are probably curious!

However, as Christians we are here for a purpose not only in the workplace, but in all the contacts we make with others. Primarily, our witness must be observed in the way we work. If our 'output,' if I can put it like that, is below par, not done efficiently or too slowly; if we talk too much, take that extra long meal-break, are regularly late for work and so on, that cannot possibly help a Christian witness. In fact, it would be a repellent! Incredibly, as a young Constable, early in in my career a certain Sergeant took me aside as I brought in a prisoner I had arrested for theft and reprimanded me because it was now some minutes before the end of the shift… 'Don't ever do that to me again! You never bring a prisoner in just before booking-off time; you wait until the next shift comes on duty!' Whoops!

Yet if our ability is high, working hard through a busy shift, innovative where that is possible and doing all things with determination, then we are already in a position to show that Christianity is something tangible, worthwhile and available. If I had brought to the Station any prisoner, or, indeed some-one who is lost or ill, from that stand-point that we can pray for and be alert to any openings to speak of our faith and, when prompted by the Holy Spirit, to offer the challenge of commitment to the Lord Jesus. Our witness, at work anyway, may not be verbal at all but our attitude to the work we do and towards our working colleagues may be the launch-pad for a meaningful conversation at a later stage.

Central to any witness in the work-place is the fantastic promise found in Ephesians 3.20 about our prayer life 'To Him (the Lord Jesus) Who is able to do *immeasurably more* than all we ask or imagine according to His power that is *at work in us!'* As Jesus said to His disciples, we are His witnesses wherever we are and, in the workplace, we are alongside non-Christians more than in any other place outside of the home.

I am glad to say that I am still in contact with many former colleagues.... bosses, fellow PCs, Sergeants, Inspectors , senior Chief Officers etc. and, indeed, with those whom I served. There is real camaraderie in the police service (indeed, I expect that is the case in many other professions and work-places). To illustrate this, I had a telephone call from the wife of a former Chief Superintendent [when he was a sergeant, I was under him as a constable in New Scotland Yard and later alongside him, both of us as Inspectors] who had mentioned in their Christmas card that her husband wasn't too well. I wrote in the New Year and three days later had a phone call from his lovely wife to talk about Harry and to show her gratitude of our prayers for them both.

Never be surprised – but be ready - when the clear opening to explain our faith or to explain the Gospel occurs. Some years ago, following the Annual Meeting of the Christian Police Association, an Assistant Chief Constable, who few of us knew, had been asked to stand-in for the Chief Constable of Leicestershire who had another engagement. I was with our President, John Williamson, the former Chief Constable of Northampton and the CPA Secretary .The four of us walked with the Assistant Chief who said that he had enjoyed the Meeting and that he attended a Methodist Church on occasions. Then one of my colleagues said, almost casually, 'Are you a Christian then?' It began a friendly conversation as we walked along the road but the four of us stopped when the Assistant Chief said something like, 'I doubt I could explain my position as did the speaker in the meeting. I only wish I could? With that, John Williamson began to speak about a personal and meaningful faith and invited our ACC to consider a full commitment to Christ. We stopped, I remember, on a street corner as he prayed out loud, in confession and invitation to the Lord Jesus to come into his life. I should add that as the ACC progressed in the Police Service, he became Chief Constable of Greater Manchester! And what an example he set not only for his excellence in the Police Service but his great example of a born again believer! I was at his funeral some time later and many of us who served under him shared our common respect for him, his leadership and his Christian commitment which riled at Police Committee!

Reflection: When we are 'at work,' colleagues see us as we really are. Do we join in criticism of the 'bosses' or of other colleagues? Do we really do a good day's work for a good day's wage? Do we camouflage our Christian belief? Do we pray for our colleagues? So, if we are employed, think about our attitude at work – what could we do/not do - to help people see Christ in our actions?

NB. It must be recognised that many, today, are not in regular employment either through redundancy or lack of opportunities in local work situations and, of course, it may be a health issue or retirement through age. It does mean that there is no regular contact with fellow employees though regular attendance at the Labour Exchange may mean meeting some people quite often. Christians in these situations, it must be said, are liable to be down-hearted, perplexed and being at a low-ebb, not accepting the situation willingly. Nevertheless, what an opportunity through prayer and acceptance of the circumstances, to keep right with God and have an attitude which is positive, even cheerful, which in itself is a witness to others without a Christian faith. It may sound rather glib to say that 'in all things God works for the good of those who love Him... in order that we may conform to the likeness of His Son (Romans 8.28/29) but to have that knowledge means that our God understands and can still use us in His way.

Prayer: Help me to be aware of other people's needs and with that understanding, to pray for them and to be available to give practical help, advice and support. Lord, may there be natural openings to speak of my faith and share that with them too as You direct. Amen.

Chapter 7

In sport?

How do we use our leisure time? No doubt we could have a meaningful and satisfying hobby; maybe it is having a lovely garden (at least in the Spring and Summer!). Perhaps we are keen on walking either in a walking group or with family members. I am one who likes sport and while in my younger days, athletics, rugby and cricket took much of my time from school days until I was in my forties, I still kept a good interest and kept old friendships.

Sport has its own challenges as well as excitement and exhilaration but in whatever the game, there is always a natural camaraderie. Having been a pupil at Reigate Grammar School, Surrey, I played rugby for my Old Boys – Old Reigatians – and because of my height (6'5') as a needed 'candidate' not only because players were in short supply but upper-age was telling for some. I was selected for the 3rd team almost immediately. When we had an away fixture, the First XV and the Third XV travelled together and, similarly, the second XV and fourth XVs were together; the fifth team had fixtures whenever there was opportunity for the 'older' old boys!

In that first season, after leaving school at the age of seventeen, we played many 'home' games and travelled to the 'away' matches in the south of England. After some weeks in the 3rd XV, we had a difficult match ahead at Lewes in Sussex but en route, in the coach, the 1st XV captain sat next to me and with a wide grin said, 'Robin, you're in the First team today as John has broken a bone in his foot. Are you OK with that?' 'Mike, wow, if *you're* OK with that, nervous as I am, certainly I'll do my best and pray that I'm up to it.' I was the least mature and less bulky of the forwards but enjoyed the muddy challenge, even to scoring a try under the posts! After the game, Mike came to me in the dressing room and said something like 'Well. Robin, your prayer was answered; well done; keep your position in the 1sts certainly for the time being.' I never lost my place until I joined the Police Service! Then, as a young constable, even up to the rank of Inspector (aged nearly forty I was playing this great game! I mention this because I think that many of my school mates knew I had been converted at a Crusader Camp at Studland Bay in Dorset. A number of my school chums went to Crusader classes in or around Reigate so I wasn't a lone Christian. I was, perhaps, a little shy about it when I left school and playing rugby amongst men, all of whom were several years older than me. The temptation to drink pints of beer was not very strong even though after a hard game, thirst was the first thing to be quenched. However, speaking of my faith then was not easy; I believe I was very coy and probably – regretfully - missed many opportunities open to me. I suppose I would have prayed about this but, sadly, there may have been many who knew me on the rugby field as a player but not in the pavilion as a Christian. Nevertheless, it must be said that being a Christian is not always , or at least primarily, about speaking of our faith; much more is pertinent in the way we live, the language we use and a general attitude which speaks volumes of what we believe.

Playing golf is quite a different matter in that one is with either one, two or three others for more than three hours. Ability to play is one thing; how one reacts to a bad shot either by one self or a partner is another. Some golfers lose their cool, swear, throw clubs etc. though most just accept that is always part of the game… the good, the bad or indifferent round. Yet, at the club where I play, there is rarely a day which goes by without some reference to my faith; normally something like, 'Watch your language, Robin's about!' or 'Sorry, Robin, I didn't know you were so near' when someone has sworn or told a ghastly joke.

A surprise came at my local club in the midst of a competition when walking from the fifth green to the sixth tee, my playing partner said to me, 'Robin, what has Isaiah 53 got to do with Jesus?' Wow, what a shaker in the middle of a round of golf. Of course, there is no quick answer to that and to explain fully the connection, but my heart leapt to hear such a question which I began answering for most of the rest of the round and since. I recognise that a Christian, if he or she are 'too bold' in their witness may lose friends if we continually speak of the Lord Jesus and I would understand their avoidance because no one wants to be preached at! So, I guess, there may be some truth in that attitude. Anyway, I wasn't there to preach but my golf colleague, asking about Isaiah 53, and I are still good mates! By coincidence, Chris, my wife and I were respective Captains of the Women's and Men's Sections in the Golf Club in the same year!

Up till recently, we played golf with a Church Society (the church to which my daughter Judi and her late husband Matthew attended) in Cheshire) – where many are Christians but who are encouraged to invite other golfers who are not church-goers. New friends for us and, I guess, for many of the invitees but they all know the origin of the Church Golf Society which is to share our faith as well as playing the game.

You may know that I have written books, initially about our family's reaction to the murder of our son, Stephen, who was a police officer in Greater Manchester, and two others on a less serious note using policing anecdotes. One of my golfing buddies, David, had heard about the fact that I had a son in Greater Manchester who was murdered in a terrorism incident and that I had written about it and our reaction in the family especially by my daughter-in-law (Steve's lovely wife, Lesley) and their the children. My colleague wanted to know more and we spoke about this in the clubhouse. Unknown to me, he went to the local Christian bookshop in Shrewsbury and bought 'Father Forgive. How to forgive the unforgiveable'. He then might have been my agent for the way he suggested that others should buy the book - which many did - so, in a roundabout way, they could not say 'You never told me' since the book also explains clearly the way of salvation by believing in the Lord Jesus Who loved us and gave Himself for us.

So, in recreation, there is opportunity while playing, or in the dressing-room or relaxing in the club-room. Of course, in representative sport at County or international level, there are many, many strong Christians who are quite unashamed of their faith and, whenever possible amongst fellow athletes and in the media, are clear about the difference it makes to life by believing in and trusting the Lord Jesus.

What is so encouraging to me and, I guess to others too, that a high number of professional sportsmen and women are clear about their Christian faith. For instance, Bernhard Langer, the German golfer, instigated the Wednesday Bible Class (always the evening before the 4-Day Tournaments) which were well attended by professional players and, where possible, their respective wives, caddies and others who wanted that fellowship. Then, the newspapers seem to be anxious to name Christian players in the soccer leagues, in County and International cricket and in athletics especially competing in the Olympic and Commonwealth Games.

Please understand that I am not encouraging anyone to be an overt missionary in any of these activities. What I am trying to say is that to live for Christ is an everyday, and everywhere, experience so that when somebody asks us about our faith, or seeks to become a Christian, they know who to ask by the way that we live, the way we react in adversity and that we have an approachable attitude which means being a good listener. Not be ashamed!

Reflection: Sport, in whatever guise, is a great pastime either as a participant or a spectator; we occasionally hear of players who are clear with their Christian testimony and are not shy to be known for their faith. Can that be said of us?

Prayer: What it is either to play and be involved in sport or be a spectator understanding the sport/game and knowing some of the participants. Times have changed so that Sundays are often taken up with sport both from school teams and, of course, for adult sports. Not an easy one for a Christian, Lord, but help me not to be judgmental but to take an intelligent interest in support to maintain a friendship.

Chapter 8

In the church fellowship

There have been churches – sadly, quite rarely - where there is a large-print notice in the pulpit saying, 'Sir, we would see Jesus.' quoting John 12.21. In other words, whoever has the privilege of preaching in that church, the desire is that in all that is said, please also speak about Jesus. Oh that this would be printed in large type in *every* church pulpit. Of course, it would quite wrong and a hideous mistake, to try and judge whether the folk with whom we worship share the same faith or not; or to challenge them all to understand the Gospel, or whether they read the Bible at home or not. As a fellow parishioner or member, how on earth should I challenge any as to whether they recognise the injunctions in Scripture about being the witnesses of Jesus. I don't think, however, even though I am not a minister, that I should be shy within that group to share my testimony at an appropriate time or share the Gospel and my faith and to pray that all who are committed Christians would be overt in their faith and seek opportunities to speak about it. Having said that, surely it is the church's responsibility to spread the good news and I believe that what Paul says in 1 Corinthians 9.22 – 'that by all possible means, some might be saved.' If we belong to a church which satisfies a few regular and devout people without concerning itself about the majority of folk who never darken the door of a church, then surely we must pray that there might be a drastic change that we who attend and those who lead and preach, might have a heart-felt concern that the neighbourhood and others that our faith is not just for the few in attendance. 'Others, Lord, yes others… let this our motto be.'

I was reading recently a biography of Smith Wigglesworth, a nineteenth and twentieth century evangelist and it spoke of a man of very humble beginnings who started work pulling turnips aged six because his family was so poor and of his depleted education - yet as a young man who realised that simply attending church – which he and his parents did each Sunday – meant nothing until, dissatisfied with weekly repetition of words in a book, he prayed and prayed until he 'met' with Jesus and had a life-changing experience which began a long ministry speaking of his Saviour and witnessing to a huge number of people turning to Christ. The biography has one outstanding paragraph which grabbed my attention. Here it is:- *'The reason the world is not seeing Jesus is that Christian people are not filled with Jesus. They are satisfied with attending meetings weekly, reading the Bible occasionally and praying sometimes. It is an awful thing to me to see people who profess to be Christians as lifeless, powerless and in a place where their lives are so parallel to unbelievers' lives that it is difficult to tell which place they are in, whether in the flesh or in the Spirit.'*

My word, that's a real challenge! Is this also a commentary of some churches and attenders today? I venture to suggest that it could well be. Which may be part of the answer as to why congregations are willing to continue as they are, despite no evident conversions! I recognise that that sounds rather terse and maybe accusatory but since my dream, it has been such a challenge for me to tell people about Jesus that I am anxious that other Christians have the same intense desire. If our Christian faith means much to us, why not share it wherever and whenever we can?

I cannot see that as Christians we should be silent witnesses! I guess that most church attenders might agree with that although they could struggle, like I did at Training School, to explain how they were converted and how then to put any sort of witness into practice. Some would expect the minister to be responsible for that – after all, the minister has been trained at College and is expected to share the Gospel with others. But I would argue that, using the police service a prescription, in whatever rank, whatever specialism, whatever area or community, each has the responsibility to act as a trained officer whenever and wherever called upon. Yes, sometimes, it is difficult but a constable can always call on a colleague or a sergeant to advise and assist. Likewise, a sergeant might call on his counterpart Inspector and so on in the ranks.

So, in the Christian life, we can and should also seek help and advice from one another. How would it be if an unbeliever came to us, knowing of our attendance at church, and simply asked, 'How do I become a Christian?' and we give them a spurious answer, or say 'I don't really know'. What help would that be? Even saying 'Come to church' may not be the solution!

How embarrassing! Surely, if we are a praying church, we would have some clue as to how we should respond.

Alright, the minister or church leader does have a huge responsibility with his or her congregation. In leading services, preaching the Word and teaching us in the pew, that's where we should learn how to be His witnesses. Opening the bible, bringing to life some of the more difficult passages but there should be more than a presumption that we who sit and listen, are in fact being taught to be active disciples. I believe that the pulpit should be a place of challenge to unmotivated believers and to shy Christians to put into practice what is being preached. Incidentally, I believe there should be a regular challenge thrown out to unbelievers about full commitment to be a disciple of Jesus. Surely, a minister, pastor or church leader should never assume that every listener is a committed believer!

The old hymn is rather stark in its wording - 'There's a work for Jesus ready at your hand; 'tis a work the Master just for you has planned.' So I could never issue a command, as I would as a senior officer in the Police, to go out and witness but I would advocate that those in the pulpit should explain Scripture not only eloquently but reasonably simply which (i) teaches for maturity what we should be learning from the Bible and (ii) also explains the way to put such teaching into practice. Jesus said to His disciples – and I recognise this is for believers today - ' All authority in heaven and earth has been given to Me. *Therefore,* go and make disciples of all nations...' Matthew 28.18,19 and again in Acts 1.8 'You will receive power when the Holy Spirit comes on you and you will be My witnesses...' So there are three very important words here used by Jesus Himself : He gives the AUTHORITY, to GO and make disciples. This is the purpose for us as believers. Then added to that authority to go, we don't do it on our own - we are EMPOWERED by the Holy Spirit to be His witnesses. Who are we as Christians to deny this authority and fail to go and make disciples?

This, of course, makes the effectiveness of our witness dependent on being filled with the Holy Spirit. We should not be afraid of that; once we have asked the Lord Jesus to be our personal Saviour and Lord, He promises to empower us to be His witnesses wherever we are. To be labelled simply as a church-goer without any other evidence of a changed life surely is a label none of us want but I do think that in a rural community, there are difficulties in local witnessing because we don't want to put friends and neighbours off from believing the Christian way of life. Somehow, it is so much easier to share one's faith with a stranger than with someone we know and live beside. Yet the corollary to that is that if our neighbours and villagers see something about our lifestyle and conversations as well as our regular church attendance, they might well ask, 'Why? What is it that makes you like you are?' Wow, what an opportunity that would be.

Having said that, it should not absolve Christians from being willing to speak about and share with others what their faith means to them and even bring them to a point where they can comfortably ask, 'Would you like to become a Christian?' How many people are there in everyday life who we as Christians meet and live amongst and who on their death-bed could mumble, 'You never told me!' What a dreadful and red-faced shock that would be.

What I am going to say now may be rather delicate and it is not written with any animosity but I am sure that the comments should be considered as worthwhile since, I am sad to mention this, many who have regularly attended churches of any denomination but could at the end of their life say to the ministers, 'With all that you said from the pulpit, you never actually told me that I was a sinner; that I needed to acknowledge that and confess my sin; that I should invite the Lord Jesus into my life.' Surely those of us who have the privilege of leading church services and preaching, have a huge responsibility, as well as leading in worship, to explain clearly what the Bible teaches. There is so much to learn – and to make sure that the challenge of the need of personal salvation is regularly given.

When I lived and worked in the Isle of Man, the late Bishop Noel Jones met with me and asked about my speaking at public meetings, some of which he had attended. 'Where did you learn to speak so confidently?' Little did he know then that I was always nervous when I stood up to speak, whether in a secular meeting or in a church situation. NB. Please do not think I am boasting in any way; I simply answered the Bishop's question which he felt could be of use to lay-readers and curates. I was able to tell him that after my conversion, a new local Methodist Sunday School asked my sisters and me to help and early on in that commitment I was invited to open in prayer. You would never guess now but my heart began to pound harder than it should; I began to sweat and my voice seemed to melt away. I did it but very falteringly, hoping never to do it again. We have to start somewhere!

I mentioned this to the Bishop that soon after that embarrassment, I was introduced to another church where there was a lively Christian Endeavour Church Club, dozens of teenagers learning of the Christian faith and how to stand up and speak about our testimony. It was so helpful. The minister of the church, the Revd W.G. Channon, instructed us and gave us opportunities to speak for an allotted time, to lead in prayer and how to read the Scriptures in church. What a grounding this was. Young people together... many of whom went into Christian service.

Bishop Noel said, 'I was given some instruction while at College training for the ministry but was never given enough advice or time to practice delivering a sermon. I note, Robin, when you speak, you have notes but don't stand up and read them; I can see that the notes are there from your preparation but while speaking the notes are just an aide-memoir as you keep your eyes on the congregation.' Can you help my Curates and Lay Readers to do this?

I explained to Bishop Noel that in the Police Service, as an Inspector with others at the National Police College, we had tuition on public speaking and later, on the most Senior Course before taking the highest ranks, another intensive course on public speaking – preparation, theme, illustrations, conclusion etc. So that when I arrived in the Isle of Man, and met with and prayed with the Bishop, it was then that he asked me to 'teach' prospective Lay Readers, and Curates, how to speak and preach and how best to publicly read the Scriptures and pray extemporaneously. I was not immediately jumping at the opportunity but, perhaps falteringly, I thought, 'What a privilege and, indeed, a challenge!' And so a new venture in my life began!

All that the training gave me, at least, was some ability in public speaking and also how to think on my feet especially with the media, press conferences or with the Police Committee. But, surely, this is not just for police officers – what a grounding for all Christians so that we are not floundering when asked to share our faith, when listening to people who have some crisis or other or, incredibly, when someone asks us to introduce them to the Lord Jesus and the Christian faith! If you ask some of the members of the church in Port St Mary to whom I passed on to groups in 6 week sessions - much of what I had learnt and then 'translated' to church members most of whom would tell you that it helped with conversations etc outside the church context - viz speaking with neighbours, work colleagues and so on. The course for Lay Readers and Curates was modified for members of the church congregation and what a huge difference it made in worship.

Should not church be a training ground equipping us to live for and speak about our Saviour? Yes, we all are a little nervous but if we are too shy or ill-equipped to live for and speak of our faith, so many of our friends, neighbours, work colleagues etc. could at the end of life rightly accuse us of silence... 'you never told me! [Remember my awful dream?] Why?' How despondent we would be if our Christianity was confined to sitting in a pew or on a chair- yes, enjoying the worship, reading and what was said from the pulpit - if and I say it again, they confronted us and said, 'Why didn't you tell me?'

When I first was accepted as a Local Preacher, I had learnt from my Pastor while amongst the young people, that preaching can be confined to I P A and double C. You might ask what that means, simple dot com. I = Introduction; P = presentation;

A = application and C = Challenge and Conclusion. I explained this in a private conversation with Bishop Noel and his response was quite surprising, 'If only I had known that!' (he had been a senior Minister in the Royal Navy). He continued. 'It would have been such a help in preparation on a ship and now as a Bishop! I think I'll pass that on to my ministers and curates!'

Reflection: It is really important that we need to ponder where we stand – concerning our conversion and salvation. Whether we are 'private' about our faith? Whether we gladly attend church services but shy away from talking about it to others who don't attend church? In some instances, witnesses to a crime may be compelled to attend court in a trial because their evidence is crucial. We are not compelled to be in church nor are we compelled to be His witnesses – but our faith is crucial, not only for us but for others who as yet have no Christian belief.

Prayer: Lord, please help me to be a willing speaker or to simply explain my conversion and Christian life so that others may be encouraged and be used in Your service.

Chapter 9

The tools

If we worship in a lively church, there will probably be some form of overt witness. For example, some churches like to have a fairly large Notice Board – once known as a Wayside Pulpit - on which at various times there will be biblical promises or challenges for passers-by to read and hopefully digest. That also begs the question that if someone asks us what it means, we should be able to reply lucidly or, even be honest, and say 'Well I don't really know but I can get someone to be in touch with you to explain.' Provided that the notices are not crude or condemnatory, surely they provide at least, a talking point and, maybe, give an opportunity for passers by and non church-goers to think about their own lack of faith. On this topic, if a church has a regular member who is artistic or a local artist is willing, the Noticeboard – though silent – is a wonderful read and talking point. Of course, if an illustration is depicted illustrating a verse of Scripture, so much the better. Some churches call it the Wayside Pulpit so what an opportunity for all passers-by to read, ponder and even ask a church member what it means.

There are some churches which simply advertise the times of services; no problem with that except it begs the question as to why a non-believer should want to know when services are being held. Personally, I think there is a place for at least two large notice-boards - one for the 'message' and the other for the times of 'operation'.

This is a real conundrum. If it is possible, endeavour to have some church activities away from the church building itself. And why? It is amazing how many folk have a real aversion to going inside a church building unless it is to examine the architecture or the stained glass windows or to hear their Bans of Marriage read, then be married or, too late, their funeral! Yet the same people will willingly attend a church wedding, a baptism of an infant or, at the other end of the scale, attend someones funeral.

I am regularly invited to speak at Men's Breakfasts, even clubs and Evening Mixed Dinners – even lunch-time speaking though those opportunities with limited time of course. Most of these events are not in the church or church hall but in local restaurants or hotels. I like to chat while the meal is being served and eaten and quite frequently hear people at table saying something like, 'So glad this is being served here in this hotel.' 'Why?' I might ask. 'Because the food is professionally cooked and served and it is on neutral territory.' Please, I am not decrying such events in a church hall because many of those to which I have gone are successful and, presumably, satisfying to the church and those invited and I have to accept that being in a pub or hotel is probably more expensive but invited guests generally prefer not to attend a gathering in a church-hall.

Having mentioned these meals, I hear many responses when I announce the next Men's Breakfast to be held locally; some men who regularly attend church will respond, 'Oh no, that's not for me.' or 'Wait a minute Robin; my faith is private.' or 'I don't know anyone with whom I would be comfortable inviting them to a church event.' That, to my mind, is very sad; I believe that attending such an event is possibly the only opportunity there is for guests to hear the Gospel; this form of evangelism is simply inviting some friends to breakfast or dinner! But such a response could easily be challenged ' You are right, it is not actually for you. It's for those men you could invite!'

As a live illustration, I remember attending a Men's Breakfast and the organiser mentioned to me on the telephone that I would be sitting opposite a retired Admiral who had been converted at the last Breakfast. Sitting next to him will be two men and next to you will be two more men, none of whom were church-goers. 'The Admiral is so full of his new-found faith, he will look you in the eye and tell you all about his life and conversion while the four men there will have to listen!' And that scenario did occur and the Admiral, obviously used to speaking and holding the attention of others, was very artic-ulate, amusing and interesting especially when he said that although in the Navy he had often heard Padres speaking at formal services, he never could remember being challenged as to his lack of faith. The four men at our table listened without butting in but were ready to ask some very interesting questions afterwards. The Admiral had no answer to some of the points since his faith was very new but it didn't put him off and, from comments afterwards, none of those others at the table were 'put off". This was evangelism from the 'horses' mouth!'

Oh that we who profess to be Christians would be so excited about our faith.

Changing slightly but again about activities to which men, women and young people can be invited, there are courses such as Alpha and Christianity Explored. They are merely examples and there are other courses with a similar aim to explain the Bible, the Gospel, why Jesus came and so on. These, too, can be held in churches or church-halls but in my experience, the more warmly accepted are such courses being held in homes. Starting the event with a meal and, maybe with a video afterwards, is a superb way of leading people to a commitment to trust Christ. When I was in the Isle of Man, every Wednesday morning at 7am a dozen or so men met for a bacon bap and cup of tea or coffee and spent the next hour or so talking about their new faith and how to live a Christian life… then off to work. Each of the men had been converted through the Alpha Course, with such an exciting start to their Christian life. In any of these activities, few who attended would be able to say 'You never told me' because it was difficult to hold such men of faith back! They, then, became the witnesses without a dog-collar!

Sadly, Sunday Schools have been in decline for a number of years mainly because daily life has changed so much what with shopping, sport, other secular activities that now make Sunday another week-day. Older children at school have homework and/or sport during the weekend so they are difficult to reach. Younger school-age children, however, can be encouraged to an early evening or Saturday morning activity with a view to introducing them to the Christian faith in a simple way. And in school, some head-teachers welcome 'Open the Book,' viz.

Church members acting out Scripture which, it is hoped, will mean that teachers watch and listen and parents will hear about when their children arrive home.

Somehow, what were once known as Family Services at church - maybe for once a month in the morning - rarely attract families! Generally, the Family Service has the same congregation as at the regular services although one way of reaching parents is to specifically ask some young people to come to the Family Service and read, or sing, or even dance – at least, to introduce something different from the normal worship service. I remind you again of Paul's words in 1Corinthians 9. 23 'that by all possible means, I might save some.'

On another tack, I know of some churches who have Walking Groups – the participants being a core from the local church but many others who are not churchgoers but enjoy the open-air and the company. In the same context, I have come across church Model Railway Clubs; Knitting Clubs; Wood Carving Groups; Book Reading Groups (study a book and then discuss it together) and other activities where there is at least some interest or inquisitiveness within the congregation who are willing to share their faith. There are churches which run a Golf Society, and other sporting interests as outlined above. As said by some saint, 'Imagination is the key!' Or as I have heard, ' We will outreach by all possible means!'

Surely, the local church should be the starting point, the place of teaching and reaching, the place where fellowship is strong and where we encourage one another both in our united faith and our evangelistic endeavours. You say, 'Not for me?' Why? We have a treasure; we have a life in Christ which is above any other; we have a faith which is not a hidden secret. Come on!

So many churches are simply 'marking time' and satisfied – perhaps frustrated – with the status quo and the same few people turn up each week with no newcomers. A Sunday club!

It is so good to know of churches which are 'launching out' and are quite innovative where there is lively worship, warmth in friendship and fellowship, 'live' music bands, and, in addition to the sermon, a testimony or two from believers talking of their faith, maybe some of the difficulties they have at home or elsewhere, sharing their experiences. Coffee mornings are quite common but do they achieve anything more than just fellowship with the group of believers who regularly worship together? Surely, such events are an open opportunity to invite people outside the usual congregation!

A number of churches, in all denominations, are springing up and looking for 'outreach opportunities' actually answering some of the questions which I have articulated earlier ie language, especially if there are some from other countries whose understanding of English or the native language, is poor. Yes, I recognise that some church-attenders do not look for change and, perhaps, I can understand that but surely the higher motive must be to reach those who don't have a Christian faith or, maybe, have lost or deliberately discarded the faith they once had.

And what about Street Pastors? Have you thought about either joining with your local group or, at least, supporting them with you regular prayers? You may be surprised at the activities in towns and cities through the night! Alcohol is available not only in public houses but in the numerous night-clubs that there are, open through part or most of the night. Many young people – and old folk too – will invade the town and spend time in the Night Clubs, well supplied with drink and then, maybe but often the case, move on to other clubs.

One of the many problems which arise, of course, is drunkenness; or, at least, having been well supplied with drink, and then the noise, the misbehaviour, the fights and waiting around for public transport to start, maybe in another 2 hours or more! For years, night-duty police have had to cope with this behaviour pattern but another group has sprung up called Street Pastors who try to cope sympathetically by friendly accompaniment, have listening ears, supply flip-flops for ladies who can't walk on their high-heels because the drink has rendered them unbalanced! The Street Pastors are out through much of the night getting alongside the revellers and sometimes have the opportunity to begin friendships. So one of two things? Would you link up with your local Street Pastor Group or at least regularly pray for the 'Pastors' while they are out on the streets?

Reflection: Are we really serious about our faith and recognise that it is by God's grace that we have been saved? Could we be more pro-active in sharing our faith by all possible means?

Prayer: Lord, is there somewhere that I could be of use to you and thereby somehow begin to understand the deep needs of many who have no idea of what they miss by not knowing Your love and concern. Help me, Lord, to be willing to serve You somehow, somewhere.

Chapter 10

Other religions

I ought to point out that Christianity is *not* a religion at all; it is a relationship with Almighty God through His one and only Son, the Lord Jesus and the indwelling of the Holy Spirit in us who believe. It would be naïve of me to disregard other religions in the world some of which wholly dominate a nation but are helpful to those who adhere to such. It is not for me to be critical of that in any way. However, as a Christian, I would use the phrase 'By all means...' to reach unbelievers. There are openings which are more local and personal. For instance, I was involved in and invited to speak with four others in a day with senior pupils from local schools in Chester Cathedral where the students met in small groups with a Christian lady or gentleman taking the 'chair' to firstly hear about different facets of the Gospel and then have an opportunity to engage in dialogue with the speakers.

Towards the end of the day all students came together in the nave of the Cathedral, confronted by the Panel of Five - the day's speakers - and to whom questions could be fired! I was on the Panel of course and the first questioner very neatly and concisely put this to us, 'Why is it that through the day only Christianity has been discussed without any comparison with other religions?' The Chairman asked me to begin with an answer and I gulped to think of the best reply but said, inter alia, 'Apart from religions which worship birds and animals, Christianity is the only one where believers worship their God Who is alive! God's Son, Jesus Christ, came to earth, served, taught and healed but at the end of his earthly life was crucified on a cruel Roman cross but on the third day after His death, he came alive again, met and was seen by a huge number of people before ascending to heaven. So being a Christian is believing in Him Who is very much alive and promises eternal life to anyone who wants to believe. What would be the point of worshipping a dead personality or something which has never lived anyway?' There was a silence but thereafter, the students were very articulate in their flow of questions and 'arguments' but as the day finished, I wondered in my heart how many would have been really interested or even taken the step of having a believing faith in Jesus. But, it was a great opportunity for the students to hear of the living Christian faith.

Christian missionaries who have given their lives to reach unreached peoples are the real heroes of the Christian faith; men and women who have given up what some would call a good livelihood, a lifestyle of comfort to reach parts of the world still living in spiritual darkness, ignorant of the trans-forming power of the Lord Jesus and his promise of eternal life. And now, in these days, we must admit that the people from other cultures and indeed from our own, who simply do not know the true God, are actually here on our doorstep! What an opportunity for the Gospel… if only we, as believers in the Lord Jesus, are willing to speak up and live it out!

Any attempt to share Jesus with people of any other faith - or none at all - must not start with abject criticism; sometimes to be heard about our Christian belief actually means silence for a time. Listen and try to understand what is being said about *their* belief and try to recognise and understand why they believe what they do. It may take time before we can speak of the reason why we believe in and trust the Lord Jesus. This is where prayerful approaches are essential with patient listening and wisdom from God; but there is such joy when they stop, listen and consider when we speak of our faith and when some actually understand what we are saying and turn to Christ. Hallelujah!

I don't want to be too critical of those who believe in images; belief is in most cases a superstition and worship which is part of the history, the society or country where people have been born and now live; but it has to be said, sadly, that there is no 'return' except an inner relief that one has 'hoped' that something might be done for the worshipper. What is so wonderful to witness is when followers of other religions as the old saying shouts, 'we have seen the light!' To be in the company of lovely people whose life has been bound by tradition, by the beliefs of forbears, bound by belief in the existence of a power, or a god, which is actually powerless to do anything but *now* have new life in Christ. Of course it is an irrational fear inherited from ancestors and a dread of not following thereby there might be a threat of bad consequences if one doesn't adhere to its 'worship'. We really have to be sensitive, understanding and good listeners to then have the 'right' to speak about the Lord Jesus.

So, back to the original thought of this book. We could be inundated by millions of people who shout at us, 'You never told me!' 'Why didn't you tell me?' Of course, Christian missionaries who have given their lives to reach unreached peoples are the real heroes of the Christian faith; men and women who have given up what some would call a good live-lihood, a lifestyle of comfort to reach parts of the world still living in darkness, ignorant of the transforming power of the Lord Jesus and His promise of life in eternity.

When I either know from personal friends or read in bulletins about the conversion of men, women and children, especially in countries where Christianity is not unilaterally tolerated, I am really excited. I know that for some it may mean imprison-ment or beatings; ostracism or expulsion from the country but that great Scripture in Romans chapter 8 says it all, 'If God is for us, who can be against us? We are more than conquerors. What can separate us from the love of God in Christ Jesus our Lord?' Having mentioned our wonderful missionaries, we, too, if we are active Christians, are missionaries in our own village, town, country or in our schools, work-places, our sport, in our social gatherings.

Yes, respect another's religion - or lack of it; respect all people as made in the image of God, as we read in Genesis, but look for the right opportunity to share our own faith and the real life, above the ordinary, which we have in Jesus. Surely and very importantly this is something we need to pray about to fulfil the Biblical statement ' love our neighbours' and concern for others with the prayers that they might listen and or see the difference that the Lord Jesus can make in any life.

Reflection: Do you have friends/acquaintances/work mates of other religions, belief or culture? How do you view them; how do you treat them? How do you think Jesus thinks of them?

Activity: If you know of people with a different belief, pray for opportunities to do them good, to bless them, to befriend them. Perhaps you know people whose 'religion' is atheism. Commit to praying for them that they would come to know the love of God in Jesus – to know that He exists and loves them, wants a relationship with them and actually has a plan for their lives. That He died for them!

Prayer: Jesus, You said that You are the way, the truth and the life (John 14.6) Help me to help others see Who you really are. In Jesus Name, Amen.

Chapter 11

'Why?' and 'With what?'

This chapter could have fitted in earlier but I feel that its impact from Scripture is much more impelling having seen the openings which Christians could take to share their faith with those who have not considered the truth and wonder of the Gospel or have discarded it as not applicable to them. There are reasons, I am sure, to shake us into reality and recognise that we may be the cause of their limited consideration or rejection of the greatest news the earth has ever known.

When I joined the Metropolitan Police as a nineteen-year-old, fairly naive young man, I was with a crowd of men and women none of whom knew each other; we weren't dressed alike and we had come from various backgrounds in the Services, in industry, in nursing, some direct from school. I remember being the youngest in the class. The Chief Superintendent in charge of Training came to welcome us, telling us what lay ahead in the Training, much hard work in the classroom and in the ' practicals' outside etc. As he left the room after twenty minutes or so, he called back to us 'Ah, one more thing to say: 'You'll never get rich, expect the unexpected and keep your sense of humour!'

In training, mistakes were many from which we learnt; the written work meant much study in the evenings and putting law and action into one's memory. Somehow, we all managed to pass the three stages with their separate exams - and the St John Ambulance First Aid course too – and we were then 'posted' to our various Divisions in London. As we left Training School, our trainers wished us well but they underlined the essential need for witnesses – usually civilians – who have also seen or been part of an incident to which we have, as officers, been called. Witnesses are an essential part of policing but all too often, either because a witness is too shy to come to court or, worse, unwilling in the first place to say anything that they saw, thus weakening the evidence. Also, the greatest lesson, that ALL LIVES MATTER! 'Carry this throughout your career, influencing colleagues and others!

I have already mentioned that I was keen to share my faith but pretty inept at doing so. I recognised quite early in the training and then on Division, the primary object for a Christian is to work hard, quickly learn and be both assertive in some situations, a good listener always and often act as a counsellor. Yet, throughout my long police career, I was baffled about any kind of evangelism amongst colleagues and the public with whom I mixed or had to deal. Wisdom is needed of course but though I went on Christian Police Witness Teams to Churches, Mission Halls etc. where there was mutual support and a listening 'audience'. It was not, of course, quite like that on duty in the station, on the street, with the Police Committee, in press conferences, in Court etc. where care *and* sensitivity are necessary.

Yes, I kept my sense of humour... that really was an essential especially in the aftermath of some trauma such as a suicide, a fatal accident, cruelty to children or a shooting incident. Did I become rich, despite the promotions? Rich, no never... except that we always had enough to live on in the family and provide for others too.

The most memorable instruction that I stored in my brain was so simple 'Expect the unexpected'...and boy, was that true. Both walking the beat, supervising others; serving in committees, there were always surprises and it really meant that, in Scouting language, one always had to be prepared. I had learnt that a daily 'Quiet Time ' is essential to Christian living; and even at 4.30am for a 5.45am parade I recognised that personal bible reading and learning, are absolute priorities, and having a prayer diary. Added to that, being able and alert to pray while on duty in every situation, seeking wisdom, the right attitude and often recognising that listening and patience were more effective than speaking! I mention these things because the Bible outlines our commitment to Christ, our 'duty' both to Him and to others and the strength needed to be a 24 hour witness as a disciple. But I reminded myself at beginning of any duty – and in whatever rank, bottom to top – Expect the unexpected!

So 'Why' should we as Christians have to have this attitude and ability to be active in our faith? Well firstly, Paul asserts that we are ambassadors and an ambassador in life is one who represents his or her country as an envoy and diplomat. In 2

Corinthians 5.20, Paul asserts that we are 'Christ's ambassadors as though God were making His appeal through us.' I doubt there is a more compelling injunction anywhere in Scripture which underlines our calling.

But coming very close to that are the words of the Lord Jesus to His disciples following His resurrection. Called by many as The Great Commission, it is recorded that even in their worship, some believers doubted but to all His followers He said, 'All authority in heaven and on earth is given to Me. *Therefore* (note that important word) go and make disciples of all nations... I am with you always...' (Matthews 28.16-20). I take that as a command rather than a suggestion... 'go and make' disciples. I am very sure that those words are not directed exclusively to bishops, vicars, pastors or other church 'leaders'. The words of the Lord were surely meant for ALL believers and if it is a command or commission we as believers should act upon it!

We may well be regular church attenders or feel that our life is good enough as it is, in which case why and how do we expect others to turn to Christ? Let's pause for a moment and recognise the challenges in Scripture. We cannot inherit our faith or merely drift into it. The challenge from Jesus Himself to a religious man (remember that because what comes next in the text from Jesus is this, 'I tell you the truth; no one can see the Kingdom of God unless he is born again! (John 3.3). It is the difference between life and death. The passage, Jesus teaching Nicodemus, a member of the religious Jewish Council, goes on in verse 16 of that same passage, 'God so loved the world that He gave his only Son so that everyone who believes in Him shall not perish but have eternal life.' So it is incumbent on us not simply to think or believe we are Christians because of attendance at a local church. That can be like being a spectator at a sports venue, or applauding a great choir performance of say, 'Handel's 'Messiah'! So, the Bible says by inference there is more to being a Christian than being at or belonging to a church.

The Bible has its warnings and encouragements. For instance, if we actually are a Christian, 'we are not controlled by the sinful nature but by the Spirit *if the Spirit of God lives in you. If anyone does not have the Spirit of Christ he does not belong to Christ* (Romans 8.9). O.K. if He is in us and yet we feel too timid to openly confess our faith, the Holy Spirit helps us in our weakness (Romans 8.26) What an encouragement!

Paul continues this theme in another letter; 'We have not received the spirit of the world but the Spirit Who is from God. That we may understand what God has freely given to us (1 Corinthians 2.12) and, if we have been born again, we don't please God by observing high standards but we live for Him by faith – everyday faith (Galatians 3.11). We are then on firm footing to live for Him and to be able to powerfully witness for the Lord Jesus by what we are as well as, when opportunity arises, to speak for Him. Now comes the crunch – the real challenge from my awful dream, 'Do not grieve the Holy Spirit (Ephesians 4.30)'; instead be filled (that actually means a continuing 'top up' if I may use such language) with the Spirit (Ephesians 5.18). And then, the next step to realise: 'God did not give us a spirit of timidity but a spirit of power, of love and self-discipline; so do not be ashamed to testify about our Lord. (2 Timothy 1. 7 and 8).

We don't witness in our own strength. We are too weak for that! We may be too embarrassed for that! But as Jesus ascended back to Heaven, He said something so simple yet so powerful, 'You will receive power when the Holy Spirit comes on you and you will be My witnesses to the ends of the earth.' (Acts 1.8). When we are converted, when we really believe in Jesus, confess our sins and ask Him to be our personal Saviour, He fills us with His Spirit and that is why we should recognise that we are not alone in our Christian walk. The Holy Spirit is in us who believe and He - if we allow it to happen – impels us to be his active witnesses. We seek His wisdom as when we should speak though there are times when speaking of Christ is not the first objective. That may sound strange but many openings to speak of the Saviour are preceded by ACTION – help with shopping; help in the garden, with housework, or just sitting with someone who is housebound. What about having dinner-parties when neighbours can be invited to an evening meal? We may not even be speaking about our Christian faith but it may be the start of a more intimate friendship when testimony etc. can be freely given.

The most important ingredient – if I might use that word – in our Christian faith is the presence of and the unseen but most important and essential part of our commitment, is the work of the Holy Spirit in our witness. We cannot argue anyone into the Kingdom; we may have the 'gift of the gab' but conversion is essentially the work of the Holy Spirit. He may prompt us; He may use us but our words are meaningless in this context unless the Holy Spirit is behind our desire to reach others for Christ.

Paul's letter to the Galatian church is so pertinent for us

who believe! The ultimate aim – if I can put it like this – is to be filled with the Spirit so that He Who is love, joy, peace, patience, kindness, goodness, faithfulness, gentleness and self-control may exhibit these wonderful Christlike attributes as the basis and foundation for any of our personal witness and desire to win others for Christ. That is Galatians chapter 5 verse 22; read on to chapter 6 at verses 7 onwards and quote from the Life Application Bible: 'Do not be misled; remember that no one can't ignore God and then get away with it; a man will always reap just the kind of crop he sows! If he sows to please his own wrong desires, he will be planting seeds of evil… but if he plants the good things of the Spirit, he will reap the everlasting life which the Holy Spirit gives him. And let us not get tired of doing what is right for after a while we will reap a harvest of blessing if we don't get discouraged and give up.'

Furthermore, I have to say that if we are 'quiet' Christians, never wanting others to know of our faith, if we are church-goers but still say that 'our faith is personal and I don't talk about it,' if ever there was an apostle who could have taken that attitude by the beatings and insults that he had in life, it was Paul who asserted, 'I am not ashamed of the Gospel because it is the power of God for the salvation of everyone who believes.' (Romans 1.16). Is our attitude of not sharing our faith ignorance of the power of God or is it that we feel that the Christian faith is so personal that we dare not share with others?

Paul in Colossians 1.28,29 states, 'We proclaim Him, admonishing and teaching everyone with all wisdom… and to this end struggling (to witness) with all HIS energy which so powerfully works.' Note that the apostle states 'admonishing and teaching' everyone! No exclusivity there.

Are we not concerned that family, friends, neighbours, colleagues and so on are heading for an eternity without Christ and being saved by Him? If we have been born again by the Spirit of God, how can we not be deeply concerned for others who do not know Him? I feel ashamed for myself and for Christian believers who enjoy church and fellowship but deny the majority of people the joy of salvation and life in Christ and its promise. 'My dream 'You never told me' can be repeated again and again and again when we fail in our 'duty' and privilege to reveal the hope that we have and the promise to all who will believe not only in His Name but in the life that he can give here and in eternity!

Richard Baxter, a seventeen-century Christian known well in Shropshire but also in London and elsewhere in this country, has recorded in his autobiography, 'I have seen that there is no religion in the world which can stand in competition with Christianity; Judaism is but Christianity in the (unhatched) egg. Mere deism is the most plausible competitor but without a Mediator we cannot come close to God.'

So we as Christians, on that premise, not only have such a strong foundation but have an obligation to share it with others. Paul in his first letter to the young church in Corinth concludes with this admonition and encouragement, 'Stand firm. Let nothing move you. Always give yourselves fully to the work of the Lord because you know that your labour is not in vain.' [1 Corinthians 15.58].

Remember that Jesus said in the Great Commission, 'I am with you ALWAYS!' We are never alone; He gives us the strength to live for Him, to speak for Him and to lead others to Him.

So 'Why? And with what? Why, because we have to; why because we should want to and because we have something precious to give; why, because most of our neighbours, colleagues, even friends, are missing out on the life which is above everything and promises eternal life in the Kingdom of God. With what? Using our own Christian experience and walk with God, using the experiences we have had in family and work, showing what the Lord can do even through us and, of course, using the Word of God (the Bible) which we should be storing up in our brain and experience to be used for the sake of others.

I have mentioned the weakening of a court case by the reluctance of witnesses to give evidence, but how much worse, to my mind, is the fact that we as Christians, also fail to witness our faith, thus weakening the church, weakening evangelism, weakening ourselves and ignoring the need of those we know and meet because we fail in this scriptural obligation!

'With what?' I asked this question above. We live with the Holy Spirit – we have God – in our heart and thereby have the strength to witness; we have the backing of Scripture which, if we are reading it regularly at home and listen to the teaching in church, gives the promise that His Word never returns void… there the promise of 'a result'. We also have a testimony; if we really are born again, there can be no real challenge to what we have. If we have an experience we are never at the mercy of an argument!

We have to consider how many, many people could say to us, 'You never told me!' Assuming like me, there are more than a few, it really is a matter of getting it right with God; of spending that much more time in prayer and Bible reading – practicing the presence of God – so that we are always prepared for the opportunity when it comes.

Is it fear, embarrassment or shyness that prevents us speaking of the Lord Jesus? If I can answer that, primarily actions speak larger than words so if there is some need with the person to whom we should be witnessing, 'do the deed' and give the reason for the hope we have in Jesus! Let's have another look at this because friendship is obviously one opening we should be using and that can be evidence in many ways: praying, telephoning and sending birthday cards, Christmas cards, anniversary cards; inviting folk to a meal at home or out in a restaurant; all this under the heading of taking and spending time with friends.

Neighbours who may or may not be part of our friendship circle will have needs such as illness; incapacity through an accident; bereavements; a garden that needs tending; hedges to be cut; shopping to be done. There are dozens of openings which pave the way firstly, of exhibiting the love for others in Christianity and making openings to say why we want to help.

Then there are people we meet who we might know enough to say 'Hello' or 'thank you' viz. shop assistants; delivery men and women; at coffee-mornings; at the local Social Club; maybe the meter-reading folk and the bin men. Is there no end to the number of people with whom we converse. These are folk who may well say to us one day, 'You never told me about Jesus!'

I was at an evening when we were studying useful papers concerning the size of our congregations in the local group of churches. I think we were rather smug when we agreed that we 'are holding our own' and that despite losses through bereavement or moving house, roughly one or two others have come in and replace them. I sat there with a different 'take' on the figures because they didn't reflect the majority of people in our communities who never attend church; our complacency was ill-judged. A better statistic would have been to see how many homes had we visited in the service of our Christian faith? How many of our villagers had been converted in the last year or so? Yes, holding *our* own which, I think is rather selfish and complacent - almost perhaps, asking ' is there a fear of launching out?'

My dream still haunts me. So many people could still say to me, 'You have never mentioned your Christian faith or about Jesus.' 'Yes, I knew you were religious but that meant nothing to me.' To me is to be a Christian with the challenge to live for the Saviour, reliant on Him to give us the urge and openings to tell others of our faith and introduce them to new life in Christ. I have already emphasised that it may not primarily be about *speaking* – surely, it's our way of life which should show the difference about being a Christian – our attitude, our helpfulness to others, perhaps helping with the shopping, or with young children, visiting others in their home or in hospital; helping in the garden and so on. It may be that a simple question, 'Why are we doing this?' which may open the door to speak of our faith. The Bible suggests that we 'hold unswervingly to the hope we profess' (Hebrews 10.23)… that may be the very magnet for non-Christians to spot the difference! Do we profess our faith?!

I know the excuses which naturally confront us because I have made them myself! 'I'm not very articulate about my faith.'

'What will they think of me when I speak of Jesus?' 'My faith is very personal; I don't talk to others about it.' 'I'm sure I will lose friends if I bring religion into the conversation.' 'Oh no, we don't have a speaker at these events; we don't want to put people off!' These are considerations which haunt me.

Such excuses, sadly, are not valid reasons and deny much of the Bible which we would think we rely on; how sad to reach the end of our life and die with regrets that so few knew, through us, of the love that God has for this world and of His Son, Jesus, Who gave Himself to death on a cross so that believing in Him He would give eternal life. Here is a short indication of where we need to be and do. *First,* continually read, study and meditate God's Word, the Bible, (daily using Study notes which are easily available) and not just rely on Sunday services);*second.* be optimistic for opportunities to reach out to unbelievers and *thirdly,* know the excitement of helping others and then speaking of the Saviour.

There is a wonderful help for us in Isaiah 40.28-31 if I can adapt it on a personal front: *'Father, You are the everlasting God and creator of the earth and the universe. You never grow tired or weary. You give strength to me when I'm weary and You increase Your power when I feel weak. I hope in You Lord and You renew strength in me to help me walk and not faint'*

Also in Isaiah 55.10 and 11: 'As the rain and snow come down from heaven and do not return to it without watering the earth and making it bud and flourish so that it yields seed for the sower and bread for the eater --- *so is my word that goes out from my mouth; it will not return empty but will accomplish what I desire and achieve the purpose for which I sent it.'* As believers we have the mission and His word does not return void... it accomplishes what He desires – new life – through us His disciples! There is the promise of a result, if I can put it like that.

We have a testimony if we are really born again and not just imitators living what we call a Christian life – no harm to anybody and by being seen to attend church. If we really have had the experience of the reality of God, there can be no real challenge to what we have, If we have an experience we are never at the mercy of an argument! I think at this point it is worth considering again what the Bible – and for us too – means by 'being born' again as Jesus explained to Nicodemus in John chapter 3. It means a spiritual re-birth. Once we have understood who Jesus is, God in the flesh (se Colossians 2.9 and Hebrews 1.3), and realise what He accomplished for us on the cross – by the new birth He has given us; we recognise Jesus as the Lord of our life and by opening ourselves to Him and His power we are thereby be filled with the Holy Spirit Who gives us power to live for God and be His living witness.

How about that for God's strength when we feel we can't be His witness? And more: 'Jesus, Who is able to do immeasurably more than we ask or imagine according to His power that is at work in us! Ephesians 3.20. And again, Jesus said, 'what is impossible with men is possible with God!' (Luke 18.27).

How many, even now, might be saying, 'You have never told me?!' when we could have done even when we felt too weak, too shy or felt faint at the thought of speaking up for Jesus?

Reflection: We may feel that our witness is not very effective especially when it seems that few people want to turn to Christ or even take any interest in our personal testimony but we can remember this wonderful encouragement in 1 Corinthians 15.58 – 'Your labour is not in vain.'

Keep on keeping on! And more, 'Isaiah 40.28-31 which I have adapted to be really personal: 'Father, You are the everlasting God and creator of the earth and the universe. You never grow tired or weary. You give strength to me when *I'm* weary and You increase Your power when I feel weak. I hope in You Lord and You renew strength in me to help me walk and not faint.

Prayer: Perhaps you could use the above as a heartfelt prayer if and when you feel too faint to share your faith with others. Ask God for strength and believe He will give it.

Chapter 12

Change?

When I have spoken at Men's Breakfasts, Mixed and Ladies Dinners, for instance, I made it my practice (having warned the organiser) that after my arrival showing that I was there I would find a seat and just sit down at a table and join in the conversation; it was amazing what I could pick up, especially when they asked if I knew the speaker! Sometimes, following preaching in a church in various denominations, a common thread of opinion in conversations afterwards was not always easy to answer. In varying ways, the question is asked, or opinion put forward, that the 'church' is out of date; maybe by the buildings in which they hold services or by the dated language used. Then, occasionally, especially by younger people, the music – hymns, chants etc. - is just not suitable for the modern world. I try to explain that there are now much more modern songs to sing which are really up to date! As Christians, we love to sing hymns and choruses with which we grew up and, I think, don't worry about archaic language. But when non-christians – perhaps when they only occasionally come to church – recognise that what they see in their hymn book that it contains many songs in old-fashioned language – what a put-off! Christians are used to it of course but others are not.

It does seem strange to me that most churches talk about the Lord's Prayer, presumably quoting the words of Jesus in Matthew Chapter 5, when, in fact, He was saying, 'This is how *you* should pray'. Surely, Jesus cannot be praying, 'Forgive us our trespasses' - He has no sin in Him. It is an example from Jesus as to how *we* should pray! To be absolutely factual, the actual Lord's prayer is as quoted in John chapter 17 when it is introduced thus: 'Jesus looked towards heaven and prayed.'

He prayed for His disciples and for all believers. Of course there are other examples of Jesus praying throughout the four Gospels but Matthew Chapter 6 is Jesus's instruction to <u>us</u>, the believers, and how *we* should be praying. It is not the Lord's prayer! It is His teaching giving us an example as to how we should pray.

Critics will quote the language of the nineteenth century (or even earlier) – 'thee' – 'thou' – 'mayest' – 'wilt' – 'hath' – 'ye' to quote just 6 of the many ancient words used in the Bible and, indeed, in many Christian songs and hymns. A lady once pointed out to me, on this very theme, that a church service had been recently printed its service, including the prayers' in up to date wording and language – sadly, there was much dissatisfaction in the chat afterwards and the church did not resort to that again! In the discussion, the conversation – even with humour – was saying and a lady said to me, 'Why did the service quote the Lord's Prayer in the 'old' language while everything else was modern? (the church calling Matthew 6 as the Lord's Prayer had not! It said, ' Our Father *which art* in heaven…' and so on. 'Surely,' she said to me, 'God is Father, a person, so why say 'which art' - a word used for an object?. Why not pray 'Who is…' And that's not the first person to have challenged me on that! Then, in another context, what does 'vouchsafe' mean? It trips off our tongues quite often! On a personal note,. I sang a hymn, just before I wrote this, with the word *thee* in its 4 verses 13 times!

On another occasion (and repeated since by others in different contexts), a dignified man, recently retired, accompanied his wife and married son and his wife attending a local church and service. He was not a regular church attender but, as it happened, this was a Communion Service. This gentleman was obviously disturbed with something from that service and was quite critical. He said to me, 'I went home wondering if I heard 'right'. The minister in his robes did the service and I am sure he said something like this' holding up a wafer 'This is my body broken for you' and after that 'This is my blood shed for you.' I noted this to ask a question or two and I'm now asking what on earth did he (the vicar) mean?' Not an easy question to succinctly answer but I tried my best. The wafer, and in some churches it might be a piece of bread, *represents* Christ's body and the wine *represents* His blood shed on a cross. Jesus said these things at a meal *before* He was crucified - he was whole in body of course - and churches of varied denominations, use His words for us to recognise the cost of salvation. There cannot be any other meaning than that which Jesus was saying 'this represents My body, this represents My blood' The fellow continued, 'Please tell me why the minister bowed down in front of the silver cup and the wafers? [I've often wondered this myself!]. Then he continued, 'What do you mean by salvation?'

This was a serious and meant a long conversation thereafter! I probably didn't convince the gentleman but I have to recognise that in some matters, things that are accepted without question by churches and believers, overlook the question of old language and words the churches use in communion or Eucharist services. Why don't we get up to date and explain in terms which can be understood? I have said this again and again, 'Not everyone who attends church is a Christian' and when there are church services on radio or television, certainly not every one listening or viewing is a Christian. Explanations are surely necessary!

I have to agree with the questioners because I, too, find the old language difficult to take as I have mentioned before. I was asked once, 'Why do all prayers end with the word 'Amen?' And in that context, I hear in ordinary conversations between Christian people saying, 'amen, amen…' to underline or agree with what is being said! I concede that many Christians in the older generations are happy to use such language and I guess that leaders of churches are reluctant to try and change the habit of a lifetime. In fact, in conversation with a member of our village church, when I mentioned the language of the Lord's Prayer, she said it was helpful to her in worship to use the older language. I certainly would not want to challenge or disagree with that. Of course not. But for the unbeliever, always looking to question or criticise the church, such language immediately puts them off. It is possible to make the point that there are now more modern versions of Scripture where language is updated and more easily understood; also, that there are up to date hymn and chorus books with present-day language and more acceptable music with much truth but not always to the taste of the non-Christian or younger Christians. I remember a man saying to me that the hymn, 'We plough the fields and scatter the good seed on the land'... is rather hypocritical; he quoted a line or two of the harvest hymn viz. 'by Him the birds are fed, much more to us, His children, He gives our daily bread.' But he quite angrily said to me, 'What about the under-fed, the starving in many countries... who feeds them?'

Surely, we are not trying to persuade non Christians to use a different language, are we? I realise, of course, if we have been women and men of faith for some years, that we are used to the 19th century language of hymns and to suddenly change all that to modern versions may not be popular. Having recognised that, as this book has tried to test us as Christians, we surely must listen to the criticisms and even be prepared to change without in any way, diminishing the power of the Gospel.

Nevertheless, I feel I have to pursue the comments of others outside the church and examine their validity. So please forgive me treading on Christian toes as I outline a number of the 'reasons' why some don't want to know about Christianity. A husband and wife, for instance, having attended a family wedding in church, asked me why the priest – and some others – stop and bow to the table at the front of the church and then tap their chests. What *are* they doing and should we (they asked) be doing it too? 'Robin, are we missing something?' As one who also sees that in some churches, I can only say that it is the way that some people find helpful in their worship and it is obviously not a problem to them.

Then, again, in a frank discussion, following a Mission meeting, a group of men – some Christians who had brought friends along – asked why, when they attend their local church, the prayers are read from a book and used time and time again and not really pleading with God in updated information? I found it difficult to give a satisfactory answer because I recognise that many church-attenders are happy to have services which they recognise and with which they are happy – but what about the new Christian or people who want to understand Christianity but have not yet recognised that Jesus is their Saviour? Then someone chipped in, 'What about the most uncomfortable pews which many churches still have; is that to ensure that the minister doesn't preach too long a sermon?' I haven't a helpful answer to such questions!

In another conversation with a 'table' of men at a Breakfast, one of them said, 'Why do churches and religious pictures have a cross with someone - presumably Jesus Christ - pinned to it? Surely you all say 'He's alive' so why have Him still hanging on a cross? Shouldn't it be an *empty* cross? We see it outside some buildings, in stained-glass windows and in religious paintings; we see crosses in gold and beautifully stained wood rather than what we think it was as a rough, uncarved two logs tied together! Wow, that was quite an in-depth question but very intelligent and difficult to answer. I recognise myself as a long-standing Christian that the cross by itself is still a reminder of what the Lord Jesus suffered when nailed to the wooden cross… and, of course, after He died, was taken to a grave, and was raised by God to life again. Actually, I concede that this fellow had a strong point! In the local church where I worship, I have the same problem with a stained glass window with Christ still nailed to the cross staring me in the face. The great purport of the Christian faith is that the cross is empty

114

– Christ was taken from the cross, to a grave and He came alive again. An empty cross tells the whole fact that Christ is risen from death! He is alive!

Talking of prayer by the way, the lively and growing churches are those which hold regular prayer-meetings during the week *and* spend time with the minister, the preacher, the readers etc. in prayer say, for twenty minutes or so, praying together in preparation for the service to come. Chris and I went to a Baptist Church in Llanelli, South Wales where I was to speak. The prayer time in the Vestry was in Welsh and Chris asked the lady next to her what she had just prayed for. The lady, surprised with the question said, 'I don't know how to explain 'cos I don't understand English!' Then I preached without an interpreter so how much was understood by the congregation is anyone's guess!

My wife and I attended another church which was, in fact, the 'daughter' church of a large congregation some thirteen miles away. It was founded on prayer even before the 'church' services began or were publicised but once it was known to be a local church, the founding twenty-two members recognised the need for prayer and bible teaching. This is how we started and continued. Prayer for an hour or so every Saturday morning, then cleaning the premises prior to Sunday. Prayer before morning and evening services and a mid-week bible study and prayer-time on a Wednesday. We prayed for each other and gradually, prayer was answered when newcomers were converted, or other dissatisfied Christians from other churches came – within two years, the regular congregation was over 200 people attending and a new and larger building was designed and built! An up to date 'assembly' where God was blessing, in modern English using modern Bible translations. Is there a lesson here?

Music has been mentioned and I recognise that changes in this respect may be controversial! However, why not have music, for instance, which is not organ led? Why not have piano, wind instruments, percussion and strings? Yes, a good number of churches have updated but I hear the expression – usually in a critical fashion from some church-attenders, speaking of a more modern set-up. 'Oh, they are happy clappy' and, of course, they wouldn't touch it with a barge-pole even when it is obvious that God is working there!

What I don't ever want to do is to be critical of the established church; after all, I attend one! Of course, Christ is often the centre of the church but I do wonder when change is not sought and the congregation is roughly the same every week with no obvious growth. After all said and done, we are the witnesses of the Lord Jesus and there is surely an example to follow – that of Paul, a converted terrorist in the 1st century, who in writing to young churches said, inter alia, 'I will use all means to save some.' (see 1 Corinthians 9. 19-23) and especially verse 22 where Paul says 'To the weak I have become weak to win the weak; I have become all things to all men so that by all possible means I might save some. I do all this for the sake of the Gospel.'

Ah, yes. Of all the excuses used by non-Christians perhaps the most spoken is the 'dress' or uniform of the clergy! This is the question, 'Why do they wear black?' and a more recent question, 'Even the Archbishop of Canterbury wears black while bishops and above are normally seen in pink or red!? Surely, an unattractive dress-code is, as one young man said to me, a real 'put-off'. As I write this immediately following a BBC 1 broadcast from a Cathedral, I began to think of the many comments and criticisms I have had to contend with from unbelievers. Watching the T.V. we had a clergyman all in black, (with a black beard also!), an ounce of welcome, not a smile on his face, a monotonous man reading a 'talk' in a monotone; the Bible Reading by a young man with no expression and with a taut but probably nervous face; then another member of the clergy, a lady who read prayers in 19th century language, little if any expression – I could continue but my feelings went out to the many who criticise the 'church'. There was absolutely no incentive for an unbeliever to be grateful or any kind of invitation to trust the Lord Jesus. Presumably, the assumption was that church goers would understand! We as Christians surely have to think and recognise that the Gospel is because God so loved *the world – not just the comparatively few who attend church!*

Are these genuine excuses to show no interest or are they examples for us who believe to address, think through, maybe make changes for the important and life-changing help for others to come to faith? Sadly, change is all too frequently seen as a challenge or, if change is seen to be needed, it takes too long to put into practice.

As briefly, but importantly, mentioned before, I have been given, as a reason not to go to church - which can also be counted for not wanting the Christian faith - simply, 'Sundays'. Yes, that once sacred day of peace and quiet, being with the family, church going by many and so on has been thwarted by a complete turn-about. Sundays are now a day of professional and amateur sport, including school fixtures and other activities. Yes, committed believers do find time to get to their local church but it is a known fact that most congregations are dwindling in numbers partly because of the recreational activities but also for the fact that a number of shops, apartment stores, 'do-it yourself' outfits, are open all hours Sunday to Saturday.

Evangelism, which includes 'can you come with me to church?' is usually a non-starter because many people, families and individuals, have other things to occupy them which don't include worshipping in church. Surely, we need to be more imaginative in our outreach! I am wanting to acknowledge what has been named 'Messy Church' which, although organised by a local church in many denominations, meets *not* on a Sunday but at a convenient time mid-week though a criticism of that highlights the fact that many people work long hours during the week, or work away from home – a whole number of reasons – so a family evening, even including home-work for school children, and other legitimate reasons, cannot include Messy Church activities, despite the fact that such an activity has become popular in some places.

Of course, one of the main reasons people don't go to church on Sunday has nothing to do with the attractive alternatives; they simply don't see the point! In these post-modern secular times, faith doesn't figure in their lives. It doesn't seem relevant. They don't know who God is or they may have a skewed idea of the God of the Bible. Their thoughts about the character and nature of God may be faulty at best – because they simply do not know about Him. Surely, and I plead, we need therefore to tell them that there is a God and He loves them and longs to 'walk' through life with them.

A final question which crops up from time to time, strangely, because it is usually from regular attenders at church. It concerns the Communion Service. I have worshipped in many churches and denominations and I certainly recognise the importance of the precious Communion – or Eucharist – service. Even I as a long-time Christian still query why there is no explanation of the words of Jesus said at the Last Supper 'This is My body… This is My blood' when communicants receive the bread (sometimes wafer) and sip the wine. Soon after Christ's resurrection, new Christians were taught from Scripture passages, even before the Bible fully came together, and one of the difficulties came about in the early communion services, wishing to quote the Saviour; it was decided by the early church that it is right to declare that the bread and wine were literally Jesus's body and blood – this being called transubstantiation. That still pertains in many churches but most other denominations, in their different styles, will quote the words of Jesus but actually are saying (not with these exact words), that this bread and thus wine *represent* the body and blood of Jesus. When at that Last Supper, just prior to His arrest, Jesus's body was whole and His blood was not shed. While it doesn't take away anything of the worship, for me anyway, I do feel that churches need to explain what the elements represent. I have no direct quotations from any learned books on this but even with the due reverence that we have in Communion, perhaps it would not be undermining it if there were some clear explanation that the words of Jesus are being quoted but not with a meaning added to His utterance. Surely, please, the elements are *representative* of Christ's sacrifice.

I admit to gritting my teeth when I see a crucifix...I have mentioned this before but I want to emphasise it again - indeed, in the church which I attend you will have read, there is a stained glass window beaming down the church above the communion table depicting Christ hanging on a golden cross! Firstly, the cross was actually a gibbet in Roman times in the near east – rough wooden trunk or branch of a hewn tree. And, more galling to me and difficult to explain to some unbelievers, why is the Lord Jesus still shown as on the cross. Dear people, He is risen; the cross is empty! I know that some artists have attempted to show Jesus's dead body in a tomb... He is risen; again, I say, He is risen, He is alive otherwise we would be worshipping a dead Saviour!

One other matter which was brought to my attention came from a lovely devout lady, who said she had been a Christian for a long time but had never come to terms with the word 'saints'. In quite a long conversation she asked me why the church gives so much credence to Saints (with the capital letter 'S')? Churches are often named after a Saint; church festivals have days focussed on a Saint and there are places and railway stations (St Pancras for instance) called after saints.

Her problem was this : surely, all Christian believers are saints and even in the Old Testament, saints are mentioned especially in the Psalms eg Psalms 16,30, 31 and others. In the New Testament, in Paul's letters (Romans, Corinthians, Ephesians) and in Revelation... saints are connected with all believers. This lady had done some homework on this because she went on to say that the church honours particular people because of some great work they had done, or a vision they had seen. Her problem which she put to me was, 'Why are such people given so much prominence in the church, almost to the point of 'worshipping' them, detracting from the worship of the Lord Himself. She put all this, really, as a question to me and I have no answer as to why saints are given so much prominence even mentioning the consideration that Mother Teresa should be made a saint when in God's eyes, she is a saint like any other Christian believer. I now have to ask myself, 'Why did the early Church elevate certain people to be Saints, a practice condoned by certain denominations of the church?

Anyway, I have outlined some of the problems that *non* believers have about the Christian faith and, I fear, I haven't had the gift of explanation – we have mentioned language, posture, rituals, music and inferred that some folk may have either a genuine problem inhibiting them to fully believe or used as an excuse not to need 'religion' as they might put it.

Maybe, we are not too concerned about the lost! Probably, we have not been able to answer the queries or objections that our family or neighbours, or our colleagues have. But what if we all had the same dream that I had at the gates of heaven, 'You never told me?' Would *we* feel guilty? Are we shy of testifying to non believers about our Christian faith?

I have written these 'notes' during a lockdown with a recent epidemic. It was a Bishop's instruction not to have church services for a time but that doors may be open for people to enter for private prayer. Actually only two people – a husband and wife – came into the church during that lockdown. I wondered why only two people accepted the 'invitation' for private prayer. Sensing there may have been a problem or a mis-communication, I sought an answer and what I discovered amazed me! It said +something like, 'Well, we were not given a prayer book; how can we pray without a book?' I suppose I shouldn't be surprised because so many churches never hold Prayer Meetings where a Prayer Book is NOT part of the scene. People pray openly with their own words. Perhaps mentioning this should also give us the answer as to why many churches are not growing in numbers or much worse, are decreasing in numbers attending services. If there is no real concern that very few 'new' attenders or visitors ever attend church it is surely because we don't have a real concern for others or regularly pray, as a church, for those who have no interest. I should ask, here and now, how frequently does our church have a regular prayer meeting; hold evangelistic services: have Bible Study groups to help new Christians?

Reflection: Is there any situation, or opportunity, to which you could invite friends and neighbours, family, colleagues which might lead eventually to share the Gospel with them. Remember Paul's words, 'I have become all things to all people that by all possible means, I might save some. I do all this for the sake of the Gospel.' (1 Corinthians 9… 22 and 23.)

Thought: Are you, yourself, resistant to any change? But why? Think about your reasoning.

Change challenges us. It is, I recognise, sometimes uncomfortable. It can also have a root in fear. But what if change - for instance, in our attitude or in the way we conduct services – meant that people in our village, town, neighbourhood, in our family etc. might or could come to know Christ and acknowledge eternal life, rather than having to experience eternal separation from God? By not changing ourselves, others won't risk, if I might use that word, changing their own lifestyle and habits! Who is to blame?

It is not that church leaders will not change. As a young Christian, I was mystified that the Vicar chose to say, at the end of a service, 'In the Name of the Father, the Son and the Holy Ghost.' I immediately had thoughts of ghost stories but this was part of church language too. Somehow or other, gradually the word 'Ghost' changed to 'Spirit' and that change, gradually became the name of the Holy Spirit so change can actually happen. Surely, for the sake of non Christians who cannot accept the 'old' language, which is preferred by some churches and Christians, there ought to be more than consideration about updating the language, just as there are more modern versions of the Bible than the Authorised Version!

Prayer: Lord, help me to change where I need to change. Help me to remember that You are the potter and I am the clay. That You are Lord and God. As I take up my 'cross' daily and follow You, I know that this means that You are leading and I am following. Help me to do that and not rely on what I was once taught and have never considered a better way! Lord, please help me in this conundrum otherwise my walk with You is being wasted and few, if any, are even considering faith let alone yielding to Your love. Lord, help me now to put You first, to reconsider where I stand and pray that I will be willing to be a Paul and recognise that by any means, some might be saved. In Jesus' Name, Amen. Amen.

Chapter 13

The final response

I discovered a book some time ago, entitled, 'Through Gates of Splendour' Briefly, it described the Auca Indians in South America up to the 1950's which was a tribe in the Ecuador forests about whom very little was known. They lived for themselves and their families with very rare, if any, contact outside their little 'world'. As a tribe, it was thought that they were caring for each other but terrified of outside interference. They too had a fearful reputation! But an American believer, Jim Elliot, had read about this tribe and felt God calling him to reach them. So he found three other friends and got in touch with Missionary Aviation Fellowship – specifically a pilot, Nate Saint - to fly over the territory. They dropped gifts before eventually landing near the jungle on a sandy river bank. But there was no friendship; the absolute opposite! The Aucas murdered all five of the missionaries. What a dreadful shock to the families but, after much prayer and advice from others, sometime later, Elizabeth Elliot, wife of Jim, and Nate's wife felt God urging them to return to the tribe! What a challenge!

Would they too be murdered? What kind of reception would they get? It's a long and incredible story. In fact, they were welcomed! The ladies then lived with the tribe and introduced them to faith in Christ. Nate's son and others joined the group and wonderfully, the tribe was converted; now Nate's grandson is also joining them! Within the tribe to live and work amongst them and others in that part of Ecuador. The God of miracles at work!

Witness for us may not involve death in our country (!) though, of course, there are some places in this world where Christian witness *is* life threatening or worse! For us, it may mean a rebuff but the neighbours, the colleagues… even our family members – have the same need as the Auca Indians… salvation through the Lord Jesus.

Compared with Jim and Nate and their response to God's call, we have nothing to fear only that there may be a nonchalance, or 'I'm not interested'; or 'don't talk to me about religion'.

But, worse! there may be a final rebuke by so many, 'You never told me!' Jesus was very clear in His teaching, His encouragements and His challenges. His parables and hyperbole always hit the bull's eye and, perhaps, none more so concerning when He spoke about *our* witness and using the talents and gifts given to us I have mentioned this before but it is worth repeating. Jesus's words in Matthew's Gospel, chapter 25. 14-30 make it crystal clear. He outlines in this parable about talents given by a master to his servants just before he went away on a journey. To one he gave five talents, to another two talents and to a third one talent. On the master's return he wanted to see the result; the first two used their talents and doubled their worth but the man with one talent hid it and did not put it to any use. To those who used what they had he said, 'Well done, good and faithful servant- come and share my happiness' - what an accolade. But, and it is a big but, to the servant who hid the talent and never used it, the Master was angry and banished the servant to the point of becoming an outcast.

Yes, that is a story, a parable, but with a definite meaning for all Christians today. Being born again, we have all been given new life and gifts; different talents but all worthwhile. Jesus was challenging his followers to use the gift given to us and *not* hiding it, burying it or being shy about it. If we hide what He has given, never glad to have it or being thankful for it, just being shy or coy about our faith - then we displease the Master and may well mean that the dream I had comes true - 'You never told me!'

As far as we are concerned… and I mean concerned - that our wider family our many friends, acquaintances and others, who know the Lord Jesus personally, having been soundly converted, is obligated and privileged to do all possible to share our faith, one way or another. Speaking at our local 'Filling Station,' it was my concern after much prayer in preparation to challenge all of us who were there on this very point of Christian witness and sharing our faith. My illustration was simple - just as a vehicle – it may be our car, or any other vehicle of course – needs to fill up with fuel, or re-charge an electric battery – we then have to leave the filling station and use the vehicle. What would be the point of staying at the pump?

So we need to be filled with the Holy Spirit continually and in His power be the witnesses that we are meant to be. Each of us, as Christians, has a 'job' to do. Firstly, as the Bible says, we must willingly 'Let our life shine before others that they may see our good deeds and glorify our Father in heaven.' (Matthew 5.16). Then, remember that we are God's workmanship, created in Christ Jesus to good works which God has prepared in advance for us to do.' (Ephesians 2.10). I read of a lady in the USA who had a note in her purse as a daily reminder, which said, 'I am a work of art, signed by God. Never will there be another person just like me and therefore I have a job to do in this life that no other can do.' As the hymn writer put it, 'There's a work for Jesus ready at your hand; there's a work the Master just for *you* has planned.'

The incident in the New Testament which is called the Feeding of the five thousand.' (it is actually many more than that if you read that wives, mothers and children are also included in addition to the five thousand men). A young lad brought his lunch of bread and fish and gave it to Jesus who, after He blessed it, fed the multitude. We might well feel that we have little or nothing to offer in the way of serving and reaching others for the Lord; so let us give ourselves to Him so that with His blessing, His encouragement and ability, we are released willingly for His service. He is able to use us though we may feel unable or unworthy in His Service.

So, being filled with the Spirit, let go and let God! Paul, a converted terrorist who oversaw the death of Stephen, was converted and became an out and out leader in the Christian church of his day; in the many churches to whom he wrote, there was always the encouragement to reach out. Be filled and go!

To the church in Rome, 'Love your neighbour as yourself...

understanding the present time – wake up from your slumber (Romans 13.9-11) 'Each of us will give an account of him (her) self to God (14.12).

To the church in Corinth (Greece)… I make myself a slave to everyone to win as many converts to Christianity as possible. (i) to the Jews, I became a Jew to win as many converts as possible; (ii) to those under the law (ie those living with Old Testament rules outside the Christian Gospel) I became one as I once was, under the law, so that I might win some of them too; (iii) to the lawless, I became one of them as to win them; (iv) to the weak, I became weak to win the weak; (v) I have become all things to all people so that I might save some and I do this for the sake of the Gospel (1 Corinthians 9.20-23).

To the believers in the Galatian church, Paul underlines in his letter, 'Let us not become weary in doing good for in time, we will reap a harvest. As we have opportunity, let us do good to all people not just the family of believers.' (Galatians 6.9 and10). I must say that it is easier to love and help fellow believers. It is much more difficult to focus on those who don't attend our church, who are alone at home, who are ill, who need help with housework or shopping, or in the garden, or who are in hospital or nursing home and would be so grateful for a visit. There are, of course, many more examples of - in Paul's words 'every opportunity' – doing good.

Then there's Ephesus, Paul aims at believers by saying, 'Be careful how you live – not unwisely but as wise people making the most of life because the days are evil.' (Eph 5. 15-16).

To the Philippian church, our way of life is an example -viz 'let your gentleness be evident to all; do not be anxious about anything; whatever is true, or noble, whatever is right and pure; lovely and admirable… put these into practice… and be content whatever the circumstances. Let unbelievers see by our way of life, our attitude, our helpfulness, be evident all the time and live unashamedly putting this into practice (Philippians 4. 5-9).

Then to the Christians in Colossi. 'Be wise in the way you act towards outsiders making the most of every opportunity; let your way of life – and your conversation – be always full of grace – seasoned with salt – so that you may know how to answer everyone. (Colossians 4.6).

And to the church in Thessalonia: 'In your daily life, win the respect of outsiders (4.12) and 'live in peace together; warn the idle, help the weak and be patient with everyone; be kind to each other and to everyone else; be joyful always, pray continually and give thanks in ALL circumstances – 1 Thess. 5.12-16).

As said by a saint of old: 'The glory of life is to love, not be loved; to give and not to count the cost; to serve and not to be served.'

Of course, Paul was writing to believers with a church community and fellowship and, of course, it might well have been to us today. Sadly, and I am very loathe to say this, the 'church' in its widest connotation, whatever the denomination, is not the great influence as it once was and there may be many reasons for that. But, the fact remains 'We are Christ's ambassadors!' Our Lord has committed witness and evangelism to us His followers. I quote again and make no apology – 'We are Christ's ambassadors as though He is making His appeal through us (2 Corinthians 5.20).

In its literal sense, an ambassador is the highest ranking diplomatic representative appointed by a Government to represent it in another country. In Scripture, this involves all Christian believers. In the New Testament , the Greek word is *presbeuo* written literally to Christian elders or to Christians in general (depending on the context) but REPRESENTING THE LORD JESUS HERE ON EARTH. It is a high calling to believers and a wonderful privilege bestowed on us all. It also brings to mind the real meaning of witness, *martyr,* Christians willing to die for the cause! Many over the centuries have literally had that fate.

Some will remember the plastic bracelets which had printed on them *'What would Jesus do?'* which originated in an American church and spread through much of the western world. It is a big question for us all to ask - what Jesus might do in any situation.

James, in his New Testament letter asks the question, 'What good is it if we claim to have faith and have no deeds? Faith by itself is dead!' (James 2. 14-17).

The one thing worse than a quitter is the one who is afraid to begin!

Thus, I conclude on biblical instruction: Be filled; be used and do what Jesus would do! We are not alone in our witness. Jesus emphasised again and again, 'I am with you.'

Chapter 14

Afraid?

Is there a fear factor? Are we 'scared' that we might have a rebuff by speaking of Jesus? I have earlier mentioned that it is not always possible, at first anyway, to actually speak of Jesus but surely our aim is to live such a life that we are seen as positively (in the best sense if that word) different? Life in general supplies the opportunities - perhaps not immediately to actually speak about the Lord Jesus but it opens a 'channel' through circumstances to show the care, the thoughtfulness, the listening ear – the difference from not caring to being aware of say, loneliness, poverty, illness etc. thus recognising a need and being alert and ready to take action!

When a friend, neighbour or, indeed, someone we don't really know – a stranger in the street, on a bus, in a train, on an aeroplane – opens a conversation it may reveal an opportunity to help in some way revealing a problem which has troubled them. We may not actually want to have a conversation but, you never know, so listen intently as the conversation continues. In our silence we can be listening to them and actually praying for the right response when the opportunity comes. But I ask the question again, 'is there a fear factor?' Are we happy simply to listen, say a few comforting words, thinking ' there, there' without asking for God's prepared reaction which may either be there and then or later, with the real and ultimate answer to the need?

I have heard of people, and actually know some of them, who dread being in any company, don't look forward say, to being taken into hospital or to a Care Home, not because there is a problem but because it will mean speaking with people they don't know. A good friend of ours who had been diagnosed as suffering from cancer, had, for many months, to go into a hospital ward for five days every so often for aggressive treatment. When we heard about this and spoke on the 'phone to her, trying to be sympathetic, she quite readily said that she looked forward to these spells in a cancer ward knowing that there would be five others there having the same treatment and it may be an opportunity to be a good listener and, possibly share her faith. Before each of those five-day treatments, she would be in prayer asking that God would use her and open doors to be a 'good listener' and to open the way to share her Christian faith.

So my final word is the ultimate challenge. We who are born again have eternal life! Who are we to keep that to ourselves. Jesus says that we must bear fruit. *'I am the vine; you are the branches. If we remain in Him and He in us, we will bear much fruit; apart from Me you can do nothing. If anyone does not remain in Me, he is like a branch that is thrown away and withers; such branches are picked up and thrown into the fire and burned. IF YOU REMAIN IN ME AND MY WORDS REMAIN IN*

YOU, ASK WHATEVER YOU WISH AND IT WILL BE GIVEN YOU. THIS IS MY FATHER'S GLORY – THAT YOU BEAR MUCH FRUIT SHOWING YOURSELF TO BE MY DISCIPLE' (John 15.4-8).

And these nine instructions (Jesus speaking): (1) Love your enemies; (2) do good to those who hate you;(3) bless those who curse you; (4) pray for those who ill-treat you; (5) if you are struck on the cheek, turn the other one;(6) if someone takes your cloak, do not stop him;(7) give to everyone who asks you; (8) if anyone takes what belongs to you, do not demand it back;(9) do to others as you would have them do to you.

(Luke 6.27-31).

These verses, among many others, depict the life of a real Christian rather than just a church attender. We should have lives which are quite positively different from the norm and are therefore the backcloth of all that we do to help others and – when possible as a result, opens the door to speak of the Lord Jesus and His love.

Reflection. Could you be so positive in such situations to not only want to share your faith but to be a sympathetic listener? The Boy Scouts 'motto 'Be Prepared' is so apt. Most days are opportunities for people to see in us the difference and, at some stage, to be prepared to give a reason for the hope that we have (1 Peter 3.15).

My original question needs an answer – are we an active or passive Christian?!

So what's wrong... or right?

You may wonder why I have included the next few lines

concerning the commencement of 'policing' and its evolution over the years recognising that to be useful and effective, policing in its organisation and operation must be up to date. Change has been necessary through the years and continues to change even now.

In my experience as a police officer in every rank, it was rare if a year went by that there were no changes either in the law, a procedure, evidential practice and attitudes. At Training School, we learnt parrot-fashion about the origins of policing, from tribal rules regarding security and inhabitants appointed to prevent thefts, of settling arguments about property and general well-being in the early communities. This meant dividing people into groups of ten called 'tythings' under a 'hundred man' who was responsible to the Shire-reeve, or Sheriff of the 'district'.

This tything-man system, following contact with Norman feudalism through William the Conqueror in the eleventh century, changed considerably though it was not destroyed, rather, it evolved in time into something that is a ghost of today viz. the tything-man became the parish constable, and the Shire-reeve, the Justice of the peace. It had reached that system by the late seventeenth century and in the eighteenth century it was seen that one unarmed able-bodied citizen in each 'parish' who was appointed or elected annually to serve for a year, unpaid, as parish constable. He worked in co-operation with local justices in securing observance of the laws (mostly unpublished!) and maintaining order. Later that century the maintenance of order was conferred on 'guilds' or specified groups of citizens who were paid for their role especially for guarding gates and patrolling the town streets at night.

Sadly, this system began to fail and the impotence of law-enforcement became a menace to society; such that, in the early 19th century, things came to a head and the utter necessity of properly appointed police was primarily organised in London with the first Metropolitan Police Act under the then Home Secretary, Sir Robert Peel. The nick-names of police officers appointed was 'peelers' for obvious reason. The tighter organisation of officers with specific duties in London became the code for towns outside the metropolis and that evolved into policing in all areas of society.

Policing continued to improve as the population expanded and through the 19th and 20th centuries, and even now in the 21st century, improvement of existing systems was always sought; laws changed, and new laws were brought into existence as society changed. I must emphasise that policing cannot and will not stand still. It is a natural reaction and a necessary response to safeguard communities, businesses, public services and all manner of other matters for the sake of genuine understanding and commitment.

You may well ask why I have taken time to outline the evolvement of modern policing in society. Policing today is the result of change, keeping up with the times and anticipating the need for new law, of up to date training and moving on from dated procedures.

So here is the point of that history lesson! To my mind, Christian worship, membership of churches of whatever denomination, biblical preaching and teaching, Gospel presentation and personal witness must not only keep up with the times and be on the alert to anticipate the need for change. In some way, this is already happening; for example, the various translations of Scripture from the King James's version to the New International version with others alongside such as the Good News Bible and The Message. You see that some of the comments I have received when speaking at various functions that 'the church is out of date' – mainly because of its 19th century language does have some truth. Established Christians, generally speaking, are happy and satisfied with the status quo but, surely, if we are intent on sharing the Gospel and inviting non-Christian people to our church, we must be aware that there could be some mystery when they hear the old words used.

It is not only adults who share this opinion of archaic language but many young people have made similar comments. I have the privilege of speaking at College and University Christian Unions where outreach to unbelievers is hindered by a seemingly (to them) outdated religion. I guess that at nearly all the opportunities I have to speak, usually in discussion afterwards or even in some other venues, a question and answer session while I stand at the front someone will speak of the outdated language (thee, thou, vouchsafe etc.) will be raised. I have to agree with their problem and almost go along with it because I also wish that bible, hymns, choruses and prayers, were in what I call modern language.

Many churches – and I am not deliberately aiming criticism concerning one denomination – still hold on dearly to dated language. While I wholly accept that many devoted Christians are happy with the particular 'thee' and thou' and 'vouchsafe' and so on, it misses the point I am making. If we are His witnesses, we have, surely, to be able to say that Christianity is up to date. I think that many in a church where all the prayers are from a book, or quotes from early believers, it would be so difficult for such folk when they have been born again to pray in an extemporal manner, in a group prayer meeting, for instance.

There is sad evidence that traditional worship, in any denomination, while suitable for the regular worshippers, is not attracting non churchgoers either young people or adults… so that numbers are slowly dwindling and in time could fade away. A question to ask ourselves, 'How many new people have we attracted to our services each week?' We may be happy with tradition but it means little or nothing to non-church goers! Of course there are churches – again, in a number of different denominations - where there is growth. It may be a generalisation, but examine their services and you will find up to date language, lively music and songs, biblical preaching with teaching and challenge, testimonies from Christians of any age – and they are a place where newcomers are warmly welcomed and can feel at home in an atmosphere which they understand.

Traditionalists don't like change; to even speak about or discuss contemporary worship is anathema to them; they are happy to stay with their own settled services regardless of the rows of empty pews and regardless of the hundreds and even thousands who have no knowledge of the Lord Jesus and His love. Please, such regular worshippers I am not in any way condemning; they are, presumably, happy in their faith… but one has to ask about their lack of concern for neighbours, work colleagues, fellow sports people – many, many young people too? Jesus insisted that His disciples should be witnesses; Paul, a converted terrorist. wrote that

Christian believers should be ambassadors for Christ; always ready to give a reason for the hope they have. The New Testament encourages Christian believers not to be shy of their faith – ever giving a reason for the hope that they have. Congregations should be urged by their leaders not only to be instructed by preaching but challenged about witness when not in church, wherever they are.

So where does 'the church' stand on this? Is the emphasis on keeping the regular services going; the constant fear of lack of money, the weekly time together in a never-changing huddle? Why are we all not spurred to share our faith? Or, are we a bit timid of sharing our faith? Why are we afraid of change? To the young church in Corinth, Paul wrote, 'I make myself a slave to everyone to *win as many as possible.* To the Jews, I became like a Jew to win the Jews; to those under the law, I became like one under the law so as to win them. To those not having the law I became like them to win them; To the weak I became weak. I have become all things to all men *that I might save some* and I do this for the sake of the Gospel.' [1 Corinthians 9.22] In the other letter to the Corinthian church, he states again 'that we are ambassadors as though God were making His appeal through us!' [2 Corinthians 5.20].

It is sadly possible that a local church has a few people who regularly attend services but is roughly the same few week after week, month after month and so on. No growth and, sadly of course, some will die reducing the congregation number year on year. A growing church is one that has a real and active concern for non Christians; has weekly prayer-times… prayer not as printed in a book but prayer from the heart; church members who are really and actively committed to the town or the community most of whom have no idea of the love of God, of the saving power of the Lord Jesus, or indwelling of the Holy Spirit! One day, we will have to give an account to our God and Saviour and what would He say if He says to us 'NOT WELL DONE... you have not had concern for the non Christians in your family, in your village, in your profession or community.'

So back to the beginning - I had a dream which alarmed me because of the dreadful shouts and accusations 'you never told me'. That was stunningly real! I have to say to any Christian, 'don't wait for such an alarm call.' Don't be ashamed of the Gospel. To many churches, 'Get up to date and be contemporary – this is not an accusation but an encouragement to think of the unbelievers who have never been told of God so loving this world that He gave His only Son, Jesus, that whoever believes in Him will not perish but have eternal life.' How awful, how dreadful that anyone should say to us, 'You never told me!'

Without exception, anyone born has to die! Sounds morbid but it is a fact! So often, certainly in English-speaking countries, there are people relying on fate, on ignorance and they sail through life with a nonchalance and little concern, or even fear, of what happens when they breathe their last - be it prematurely through illness or accident or in old age. So many will get through life hoping that all will be well; they sincerely rely on crossing their fingers or touching wood. How absolutely absurd!

There are many really lovely people in our towns and villages;

people who enjoy life, have a great and loving family; have had satisfying jobs in a variety of spheres and, seemingly, have need of nothing yet God loved the *whole* world. Some people don't seem to need anything and neglect the fact that God so loved this world (ie. the people who live it it) that HE gave His only Son that whoever believes in Him will have eternal life. Of course there are others who are really needy through poverty perhaps, or continued illness or disability or have never heard the Gospel of new life in Christ. The Mission Field is still open!

Everyone of us, whoever we are, whatever our status or position in life; whether young, middle-aged or retired – all of us share a common need and that is the life - and eternal life - which is offered to us all by our God who, as I have just written, so loved the world that He gave His only Son, Jesus, and whoever believes in Him has eternal life so death is not to be feared!

Let me conclude with the supreme example of personal evangelism. Jesus met a woman at a well, a rather loose woman but see what happened: Pharisees – watching what was happening – asked Jesus, 'Why do you eat and drink with such scum? (Luke 5.30 NLT). Such contempt and from those who should have been the first to show love and compassion! Jesus loved people; look how He dealt with the woman at the well (John 4). *First,* He broke the rules. Jews didn't mix with Gentiles and they certainly didn't associate with her kind. (She'd been divorced five times). Jesus walked for miles to meet this woman. He went into her world to bring her into His. He mixed with her not to take advantage of her or become like her, but to reach, redeem and restore her. That's why He's called 'a friend of sinners' (Matthew 11.19). Could people say that about us?

Second, He broke the ice. Jesus talked about what she was interested in – water. We must start where people are not where we think they should be. We must use words they understand. And get over our fear of rejection. We may lose face if they say 'no' but think what they'll lose if they never have a chance to say 'yes' to the Gospel. *Third,* He broke the news. He offered her living water instead of dead religion. How can we say we love someone and not share with them the greatest thing we've ever found – salvation? Everybody we meet is hung up on the past, anxious about the future, or in need of a real friend. Once we find which door they are behind, walk through it with love and sensitivity. They're thirsty for the 'living water'. Share it with them. *(UCB Word for Today* – wordfortoday@ucbmedia.net*).*

Perhaps one of the biggest challenges to us, assuming that we are Christian believers, are the strong words in 2 Corinthians 5.14 – 20: Christ's love compels us because we are convinced that One died for all and therefore all died and that He died for all that those who live should no longer live for themselves but for Him who died for them (for us!) and was raised again. So from now on we regard no-one from a worldly point of view. Though we once regarded Christ in this way we do so no longer. Therefore, if anyone is in Christ, they are a new creation, the old has gone, the new has come. All this is from God Who reconciled us to Himself through Christ AND GAVE US THE MINISTRY OF RECONCILIATION that God was reconciling the world to Himself in Christ not counting our sins against us. He has committed to US the message of reconciliation. WE ARE THEREFORE Christ's ambassadors as though we are making His appeal through us...'

NB. An Ambassador represents his/her country in another country... we, as true Christians, represent our Saviour where we are or wherever we are sent! Or do we?

Chapter 15

Rise to the challenge!

I have stated that written prayers - some beautifully structured and even worth learning – are not necessarily the answer as to why we are not communicating the Gospel not only with our lips but also in our lives. I certainly would not like this book to be read as a criticism though much of what I have scripted are the comments people who say they are not believers because... and they outline their criticisms which, of course, may only be an excuse. I have to confess that much of what I have recorded I find some agreement. While, I know, for many Christians, repetition of prayers, written many years ago, are helpful to them. I feel that prayers written by others I often can say 'Amen' to them but, for instance, the Communion Service – being exactly the same week after week, is not too helpful. But, of course, that's just me!

Having said that, maybe the following prayers are a help if you have been challenged about your witness and testimony. In all these scenes and discussions, it has called to mind a song sung by George Beverley Shea when on the platform with Dr

Billy Graham: I haven't found it in any hymn or song book but the words are so apt and pertinent for us in our mission to others:

If I have wounded any soul today;
If I have caused some soul to go astray;
If I have walked in my own weary way -
Dear Lord, forgive.

Lord, I confess that I am not the fruitful witness that I ought to be; I am shy to talk about You and am sometimes lost for words when I ought to speak about You. Thank you, Lord, that You understand this and know me through and through. I pray for Your help to live such a life, filled with the Holy Spirit, that people will notice the difference you make to my attitude, my way of life, even coping with illness or bereavement, so that it may induce questions about my faith. Help me always to be prepared, then, to give a reason for the hope that I have.

Lord, make my feet Your feet when you want me to go where You are needed;
    Make my arms Your arms when you want me to reach out to a hurting person ;
    Make my mouth open as Your mouth when You want me to speak of the hope You can give;
    Make my heart love as Your heart when You want to show Your love and concern through me;
    Lord, make my will be Your will as I show people that You are the Way, the Truth and the Life.

Father, You are the everlasting God and creator of the earth and the universe. You never grow tired or weary. You give strength to me when weary and increase Your power when I feel weak. I hope in You; Lord, renew Your strength in me to help me to walk and not faint. [Isaiah 40.27-31]

Make me a channel of Your peace – where there is hatred let me bring Your peace;

Where there is injury, Your pardon, Lord, and where there's doubt, true faith in You.

Oh Master, grant that I may never ask so much to be consoled as to console; To be understood as to understand, to be loved, as to love with all my soul.

Make me a channel of Your peace -

Where there's despair in life, let me bring hope, where there is darkness, only light

And where there's sadness, ever joy.

Make me a channel of Your peace -

It is in pardoning, that we are pardoned; in giving to all men, that we receive; and in dying that we're born to eternal life.

And how about the words of this great and challenging hymn?
Restore, O Lord, the honour of Your Name
In works of sovereign power, come shake the earth again!
That ALL may see and come with reverent fear
To the living God, Whose kingdom shall outlast the years!

How many people might say to us 'You never told me!'

Chapter 16

Helps in chatting... know your Bible!

Finally, maybe the following might be HELPS IN CHATTING. Personally, I find using the modern versions of scripture more helpful than Authorised Version language. Yes, I have had to take time to alter my use of the verses but it is good to have the modern versions in use daily to get used to using and quoting the words...

Having said that, using Scripture in whatever Bible you might use, the following verses can be a basis for our conversations:

These are all taken from The Living Bible (Tyndale House Publishers):

God answered me and delivered me from fears – Psalm 34.4
With Jesus, a great calm – Mark 4. 35-41
Don't worry, pray about everything – Philippians 4.6 and 7
Let Jesus have all your worries and cares – 1 Peter 5.7
God so loved that He gave His Son – Promised in John 3.16
You can know that you have eternal life – 1John 5 11-13
In death, Christians have new bodies – 1 Corinthians 15. 51-57

In mourning, Christians have His comfort – Matthew 5.4

God keeps on guiding – Psalm 73.21-28

The characteristics of God's love – Corinthians 13.

Our Shepherd… we have everything we need – Psalm 23
I will never leave you – Hebrews 13. 5 and 6

Don't get tired of doing right – Galatians 6.9
Don't get dismayed – I will help you – Isaiah 41.10

Doubting: No, ask anything in Jesus' Name – Mark 9.23
Even though we haven't seen Him… no doubting – John 20.
24-29

Commit everything we do to the Lord – Psalm 37. 4 and 5

Forgiveness: Confess then forgiven – Psalm 32.5
He can be depended on – 1 John 1. 9 and 10
God remembers forgiven sin no more – Jeremiah 31.34;
Hebrews 8.12

God will instruct, teach and guide – Psalm 32.8
God's mighty power in us who believe – Ephesians 6. 10-13

No condemnation awaits the Christian – Romans 8.1
What a pronouncement 'not guilty' – Isaiah 6.7

We are accountable to God – Romans 14.12

We die only once – then judgement – Hebrews 9.27

God says 'I will never leave you' – Hebrews 13.5 and 6
God's eternal presence – Psalm 16.11

Perfect peace – from God – Isaiah 26. 3 and 4

Made right with God through faith – Romans 5. 1-5
Loving others! – Hebrews 6.11
The joy ahead – 1 Peter 1. 6 and 7
Jesus: 'I am with you – that is all you need – 2 Corinthians 12. 9 and 10
God hears all our prayers – relax! – Psalm 116. 1
Jesus will give us rest – Matthew 11.28
God will provide for all our needs – Philippians 4.19

God is able to do all He has promised – Romans 4. 20 and 21

Chapter 17

Postscript!

So what is holding us back? Why are we so shy about sharing our faith? Why does it not concern us that family, relatives, neighbours, colleagues, the sick, the dying, are ignorant of the love of Jesus and the real and deep difference He makes?

I know that many will believe the parts of the Bible that they understand but neglect those passages they don't; but what is so difficult to obey Scriptures which say, one way or another, share your faith; be an ambassador; go into the world as a Christian; pray for help to give a reason to anybody for the hope which we have in Jesus?

When we consider what Jesus has done for us from his crucifixion, when He laid down His life; that the cross is empty and He is risen and gives us both strength and, if we would only recognise it, His presence with us when we witness, surely our response should be, *'Lord, here I am, send me.'*

But what a disaster when you get to the other side and someone – or even a shouting crowd, - alleges that… 'You didn't tell me! Not just with your lips but also by your life.'

Is there the possibility – be honest – that YOU, having read this through, are still not absolutely sure and confident of your own Christian Faith? You are a regular church attender and you sing hymns, psalms, carols and pray with your eyes shut BUT are you sure of *your* salvation?

And another very pertinent point here. I have heard in various places a very similar accusation. People don't come to church. But why should they if they have not had experience of God's love for them? If people have no interest in sport, they are not going to spend money going into a stadium. If they have no interest in classical music, they are not going to spend time or money going into an auditorium to listen to an orchestra.

So why would people who have no Christian experience want to go into church? 'Oh yes' you could argue, 'they'll go into St Paul's Cathedral or Westminster Abbey and other attractive buildings, or to see an old oil painting or statue there'. Agreed, but they are not interested in sitting on a hard wooden pew, listening to old language in prayers and hymns and, sadly, not interested when people don't welcome them or give them time to chat.

And we, as active Christians, are, sadly, to blame. We Christians have the greatest opportunities in life to be in daily and hourly contact with the Saviour of the world. The opportunities to live His life in us, to know His direction and leading and the knowledge that we have the prospect of eternal life. We may also have the key to the life of others by revealing our testimony and way of living, and thus opening the 'door' for them to have the ultimate experience of the Christian life.

Have you ever prayed this and really mean it - 'Lord, use me, yes, even me!'

Having written these pages, I certainly regret any offence I might have caused by sharing criticisms from those I have met, chatted with and considered some of their concerns about the Christian faith. There certainly has not been any intention to say or do anything harmful when discussing issues which have been shared with me. And, I have no gripe about any particular Christian denomination. My hope from sharing that awful dream 'You never told me...' was the spur to put on paper things that might be a hindrance to our Christian witness as Christian disciples and matters within Christian denominations which might be the very things that non-Christians claim to be the reason why they cannot believe. I therefore conclude that there are many things in our lives as Christians which unbelievers hear and see as a reason for not believing the Gospel.

Perhaps, finally therefore, I ought to ask church leaders, whether there is enough evidence apart from anything I have written, which might be a reason for change? When I think how there was a break, long ago, from the Roman Church, called the Great Reformation – instigated by an ungodly king who sought to have the Church (if I might call it that!) to permit divorce and marriage not twice but extra times too, I have to wonder whether now is the time when Christian leaders – to include all denominations – should see another realistic and up-to- date Reformation? Is that a step too far? Or is it feasible that because of the many criticisms which people claim to be the reason they cannot believe in the love of God the Father, in the sacrifice of Christ His Son or the power of the Holy Spirit... then change should be sought and simply, the 'church,' its practices and language be up to date? After all, there are several different and modern translations of the Bible... I know that many English speaking Christians would still prefer the language of the Authorised Version and that is, of course fine, but in my experience speaking to many ladies and men who desire much more modern language and literature, something surely must be done for the sake of the world in these difficult and disastrous times.

Also, there are numbers of modern Christian songs, and surely, more to be written in everyday English?

So what about it? With today's technology, with Zooming etc. it would not be too difficult to confer. The real problem would be finding common ground for change... albeit for the sake of non-Christians – at last – being able to consider the Gospel being an open invitation for unbelievers to seek the Lord while He may be found!

If you have ploughed through this short book, brought about by a vivid and challenging dream, has it in any way challenged you to recognise that most of your relatives, friends, neighbours, colleagues at work, those with whom you social-ise or play sport... and there are so many others who could be mentioned and probably within our orbit... whose only recognition that there is a Christian religion because they see churches and you and me? Are they missing out this side of eternity of the vitality of believing in Jesus and, even more sadly, may be missing out of eternal life given only by the Lord Jesus when death occurs.

Surely, this is the time for us to repent of our failure to live out and speak out of our life in Christ. That awful day might come beyond the grave when the loud shouts echo out, loud and clear 'You never told me; you never told me; you never told me.'

Underlying all this, we have to recognise that for the majority of people, church means nothing. Otherwise they would be attending! The very building of a Gothic Cathedral, Parish Church, more modern free-church buildings and even less ornate buildings where small gatherings take place... these places are not magnets to non-Christians. Weekly services and other activities do not attract non-Christians and, I have to say with regret, while we might enjoy worship we do too little to reach out to non-Christians. I have mentioned earlier in this book the new Church fellowship in Port St Mary, Isle of Man, which through much prayer, teaching from Scripture and a love for neighbours, shop-keepers and so on, the fellowship grew from 22 to over 200 in 2 years! We now live in the United Kingdom but occasionally visit the Island; that church is still flourishing and it has, itself (although really a 'daughter' from the main church in Douglas), now established another four such churches!

One of the most startling statements I have heard – from a very intelligent and upright man – was this... 'The church has no interest for me because it has no interest in me!'

Why is it, then, that we who are regular church goers, have – it seems – little concern for the many, many people who have no knowledge of the Lord Jesus and His saving power? Very sadly, I have to admit, that we are unaware, or untouched, by the spiritual needs of neighbours, colleagues, even our own wider families. Surely, we should be literally on our knees praying for the leading of the Holy Spirit and then obeying

Him to outreach those who are sadly, ignorant, of the saving power of the Lord Jesus , Who loved them as much as He loves us! Do we not care? I guess I am as 'bad' as many church goers. We have a pattern - church every Sunday morning, same time, same place, same people. As I mentioned earlier but it is pertinent to repeat it as I end this script… when the Bishop attended a meeting of attenders of a group of churches to hear how things were going, he got the impression that - using his expression - 'we are holding our own.' It sounded that it was a matter of pride… how much better it would have been if he was able to say, 'We have some core members but it has been so encouraging to welcome several new people – even families – who have heard that our church has something vibrant; we have seen a number being converted and they have invited their own friends to come to the church services.' Surely, this must be our aim in prayer.

This actually is possible; a 'church' that cares, a 'church' that serves, a church that in Christ, saves! I underline this whole book with a suggestion… that we all read again Matthew 25. 14 to 30 – Jesus using the illustration of a master giving talents to use but which dramatically ends with one who had hidden his only talent 'You wicked and lazy servant…' What a condemnation! If we believe in and trust the Lord Jesus, we have been given much to use in serving Him by serving others. We are not looking for an accolade of our Christian life but most certainly, we have a huge obligation to live out our Christian life, to listen to and help others who have no experience of Christ for whom we should be praying regularly. It is surely pertinent to ask ourself, 'When did I last speak of Jesus to an unbeliever?' or 'When did I last have the privilege of leading someone to believe in and trust the Saviour?'

Do we not care? What will be our welcome when we meet the Lord Jesus?

But what about the severe accusation of those who will shout, 'You never told me!'

Restore, O Lord, the honour of Your Name
In works of sovereign power, come shake the earth again!
The ALL may see and come with reverent fear
To the LIVING GOD whose kingdom shall outlast the years!

THE END